MONASTIC LIFE
AT CLUNY
910–1157

Fig. I. CLUNY: THE RUINS OF THE ABBEY CHURCH: THE
CLOCHER DE L'EAU BÉNITE, THE SOUTH AISLE AND
THE TRANSEPT

MONASTIC LIFE
AT CLUNY
910–1157

By JOAN EVANS

ARCHON BOOKS
1968

FIRST PUBLISHED 1931
REPRINTED 1968 WITH PERMISSION OF
OXFORD UNIVERSITY PRESS

LIBRARY OF CONGRESS CATALOG CARD NUMBER: 68-20376
PRINTED IN THE UNITED STATES OF AMERICA

TO

MARIA

PREFACE

SUCH a book as this needs no introduction. It has neither thesis to maintain nor theory to develop, but endeavours only to give a picture of monastic life in the early Middle Ages drawn from contemporary sources. If it succeeds in making that time more tangible, and that way of life more easily understood, by any of its readers, it will have succeeded in its aim. I hope to follow it by a more intensive study of Cluniac Art.

I have to express my indebtedness to the late Professor E. G. R. Waters, Miss Hope Emily Allen, Mademoiselle E. Droz, and Miss E. A. Francis for the help they have given me on points of detail; to the Staffs of the British Museum Library and of the Bibliothèque Nationale and to Monsieur Oursel, Curator of the Library at Dijon, for the communication of books and manuscripts in their charge; and to Professor Kenneth Conant for his great kindness in showing me the results of his excavations at Cluny on behalf of the Mediaeval Academy of America, while they were yet unpublished. My mother and my friend Mrs. Murdo Mackenzie have been so kind as to read the book in manuscript.

J. E.

London
June 1930.

ADDENDA

A great deal of work has been done on the remains at Cluny itself and on the history of the Abbey since this book was written in 1930. The exigencies of modern reprinting have made it impossible to allude to them in the text; and indeed the text itself is so simple that it would hardly bear the weight of other men's scholarship. A small but pleasurable correction is for p. 120; the capitals are no longer hidden in the Musée Ochier, but are splendidly displayed in the Farinier of the Abbey, which is also developing a Musée Lapidaire of the greatest interest.

The most important development has of course been the work of my friend Professor K. J. Conant in the last thirty-six years. It has revolutionized our knowledge of the architecture of the Abbey; and we all await his definitive book which is now in the press; it may possibly appear before this reprint.

For other relevant work it seems simplest merely to produce an additional bibliography (on p. xviii) of the most important items that have come to my notice.

1968

CONTENTS

b

LIST OF ILLUSTRATIONS

b 2

BIBLIOGRAPHY

MANUSCRIPT SOURCES

DIJON. Bibliothèque de Dijon. MS. fonds Baudot 1018, No. 7, p. 111.
Mémoires concernantes les antiquités du prieuré de Marsigny (sic).
(Eighteenth century.)
PARIS. Bibliothèque Nationale. MS. Nouv. acq. français 4336, p. 97.
Philippe Bouché. *Description de l'église et de la communauté de
Cluny.* (Written between November 1793 and May 1798.)
Ibid. MS. Nouv. acq. français 6099. Papiers de Guilhermy:
Description des localités: Cluny.

ORIGINAL SOURCES

ALBERS, DOM B. *Consuetudines Monasticae*: I. *Consuetudines Farfenses,*
Stuttgart, 1900. II. *Consuetudines Cluniacenses,* Monte Cassino,
1905.
ANON.[1] *Vita S. Odilonis Abbatis Cluniacensis.*
ANON.[1] *Chronicon Cluniacense.*
ANSELLUS SCHOLASTICUS. *Visio,* in E. du Méril, *Poésies populaires
latines antérieures au 12ᵉ siècle* Paris, 1843, p. 200.
BERNARD OF CLAIRVAUX. *Epistolae,* in Migne, *Patrologia Latina,* clxxii.
BERNARD OF MORVAL. *De Contemptu Mundi,* ed. H. C. Hoskier.
London, 1929.
BERNARD, A., and BRUEL, A. *Recueil des Chartes de l'abbaye de Cluny.*
Paris, 1876–1903. 6 vols.
BRUEL, A. Visites des Monastères de l'Ordre de Cluny de la province
d'Auvergne en 1286 et 1310, in *Bibliothèque de l'École des Chartes,*
xxxviii, 1877, p. 114.
Les Chapitres généraux de l'Ordre de Cluny depuis le XIIIᵉ jus-
qu'au XVIIIᵉ Siècle, in *Bibliothèque de l'École des Chartes,* xxxiv,
1873, p. 542.
Visites des Monastères de l'Ordre de Cluny de la province
d'Auvergne aux XIIIᵉ et XIVᵉ Siècles (Nouvelle Série), ibid. lii,
1891, p. 64.
DELISLE, L. *Inventaire des Manuscrits de la Bibliothèque Nationale: fonds
de Cluni.* Paris, 1884.
(Library catalogues of Cluny.) *Le Cabinet des Manuscrits de la
Bibliothèque Nationale,* vol. ii, p. 459. Paris (Histoire Générale de
Paris), 1874.
DUCKETT, G. F. *Charters and Records of Cluni.* London, 1888. 2 vols.
*Visitations and Chapters general of the Order of Cluni, in respect of
Alsace & Lorraine, &c.,* 1269–1529. London, 1893.
DUPLÈS-AGIER, H. *Chroniques de Saint-Martial-de-Limoges* (Société de
l'Histoire de France). Paris, 1874.

[1] In Marrier.

GERBERT, M. *Scriptores Ecclesiastici de Musica*, Saint-Blaise, 1784 (vol. i, p. 247, D. Oddonis Abbatis, ut videtur, Cluniacensis, Tonarius, Dialogus de Musica, & de Musica).

GUIOT DE PROVINS. *Œuvres*, ed. J. Orr. Manchester, 1915.

HERRGOT, M. *Vetus disciplina Monastica*. Paris, 1726.

HILDEBERT OF LE MANS.[1] *Vita Sancti Hugonis Abbatis Cluniacensis.*

HÜCKEL, G. A. (ed.). Les poèmes Satiriques d'Adalbéron, in *Université de Paris, Bibliothèque de la Faculté des Lettres*, xiii, Paris, 1901, p. 49.

HUGH, ABBOT OF CLUNY.[1] *Epistolae, &c.*

HUGH, MONK OF CLUNY.[1] *Vita Sancti Hugonis.*

JOHN, MONK OF CLUNY.[1] *Vita Sanctissimi Patris Odonis Abbatis Cluniacensis.*

JOTSALDUS, MONK OF CLUNY.[1] *Planctus de Transitu S. Odilonis.*

LECESTRE, L. *Abbayes, Prieurés et Couvents d'hommes en France. Liste générale d'après les papiers de la Commission des Réguliers en 1768.* Paris, 1902. (2nd ed.)

LUCE, S. Visite par les Prieurs de Barbezieux et de Saint-Sauveur-de-Nevers des Monastères de la Congrégation de Cluny situés dans la province de Poitou, 1292, in *Bibliothèque de l'École des Chartes*, 1859, xx, p. 237.

MABILLON, DOM J. Itinerarium Burgundicum, in *Ouvrages posthumes de Dom Jean Mabillon et de Dom Thierri Ruinart*, ed. Dom Vincent Thuillier, Paris, 1724, vol. ii, p. 19. 1.

Annales Ordinis Sancti Benedicti V. Paris, 1713, p. 252.

MARRÎER, DOM M., and DUCHESNE, A. *Bibliotheca Cluniacensis*, Paris 1614; reprinted Protat frères, Mâcon, 1915.

MONTAIGLON, A. DE, and RAYNAUD, G. *Recueil Général et complet de Fabliaux*, vi, 1890, p. 117.

ODILO, ABBOT OF CLUNY.[1] *Statutum de defunctis.*

Sermones, hymnus, Vita Adalheidis Imperatricis, &c.

Vita Beati Maioli Abbatis Cluniacensis.

Un hymne inédit de S. Odilon, ed. G. Morin, in *Revue Bénédictine*, xxxviii, 1926, p. 56.

ODO, ABBOT OF CLUNY.[1] *Sermones, Antiphonae, Collationes, Versus, &c.*

Occupatio, ed. A. Swoboda, Leipzig, 1900.

OMONT, H. Deux Nouveaux Cartulaires de Cluny à la Bibliothèque Nationale, in *Millénaire*, i. 130.

PETER DAMIAN.[1] *Vita beati Odilonis abbatis.*

PETER OF POITIERS.[1] *Panegyricus Petro Venerabili Abbati dictus.*

PETER THE VENERABLE,[1] ABBOT OF CLUNY. *Epistolarum libri sex.*

De miraculis.

Sermones, hymnus, versus, &c.

PRÉVOST, A. LE (ed.). *Orderici Vitalis . . . Historiae Ecclesiasticae libri tredecim.* (Société de l'Histoire de France.) Paris, 1855. 5 vols.

RADULPHUS GLABER. *Les cinq livres de ses histoires*, ed. M. Prou, Paris,

---

[1] In Marrier.

1886 (Collection de textes pour servir à l'Étude et à l'Enseignement de l'histoire).

ROBERT, U. État des Monastères franc-comtois de l'Ordre de Cluny aux xiiie-xive Siècles, in *Mémoires de la Société d'Émulation du Jura*, 3rd series, vol. ii (1881). Lons-le-Saunier, 1882, p. 3.

ROMAN, J. Visites faites dans les prieurés de l'Ordre de Cluny du Dauphiné de 1280 à 1303, in *Bulletin d'histoire ecclésiastique et d'archéologie religieuse des diocèses de Valence, Digne, Gap, Grenoble et Viviers*. Roman, vol. iv, 1883–4.

SIMON, P. *Bullarium Sacri Ordinis Cluniacensis*. Lyons, 1690.

UDALRIC. Antiquiores Consuetudines Cluniacensis Monasterii, in Migne, *Patrologia Latina*, cxlix, col. 635.

WOELFFLIN, E. (ed.). *Benedicti Regula Monachorum*. (Teubner) Leipzig, 1895.

BOOKS AND PAPERS

ALBERS, DOM B. Le plus ancien coutumier de Cluny, in *Revue Bénédictine*, 1903, xx, p. 17.

BARTHÉLEMY, A. Essai sur l'histoire monétaire de l'abbaye de Cluny, in *Revue numismatique*, Paris, vii, 1842, p. 33.

BAUCHOND, M. Un sermon de Saint Odilon, cinquième Abbé de Cluny, in *Millénaire*, ii. 103.

BÉDIER, J. *Les Légendes Épiques: recherches sur la formation des chansons de geste*. (2nd ed.). Paris, 1914–21. 4 vols.

BERLIÈRE, DOM U. Les Coutumiers Monastiques, in *Revue Bénédictine*, 1906, xxiii, p. 260.
L'Ordre Monastique des origines au xiie Siècle. Paris and Abbey of Maredsous, 1921.

BERNARD, A. Abbaye de Cluny. Note sur les anciens Bâtiments aujourd'hui détruits, in *Cabinet historique*, Paris, 1863, p. 226.

BESSE, DOM J. M. L'Ordre de Cluny et son gouvernement, in *Revue Mabillon* (Ligugé and Paris), i, 1905, p. 5.

BOURG, DOM DU. *Saint Odon*. Paris, 1905.

BRUEL, F. L. *Cluni, 910–1910: Album historique et archéologique précédé d'une étude résumée et d'une notice des planches*. Mâcon, 1910.

BUTLER, DOM C. *Benedictine Monachism*. London, 1924.

CABROL, DOM F. Cluny et Cîteaux, in *Association bourguignonne des Sociétés Savantes: Congrès de 1927: Saint Bernard et son Temps: Compte-rendu*, p. 19.

CHAMPLY, L. H. *Histoire de l'abbaye de Cluny*. (1st ed.) Cluny, n.d. (1866). (3rd edition, ed. R. Champly), Paris, 1930.

CHAUMONT, L. *Histoire de Cluny depuis ses origines jusqu'à la ruine de l'abbaye*. (2nd ed., enlarged), Paris, 1911.

CONANT, K. J. La Chapelle Saint-Gabriel à Cluny, in *Bulletin Monumental*, 1928, lxxxvii.
Les fouilles de Cluny, in *Bulletin Monumental*, 1929, lxxxviii, p. 109.
Mediaeval Academy. Excavations at Cluny: the season of 1928, in

Speculum, a Journal of Mediaeval Studies, 1928, pp. 3, 168; 1929, p. 291 (in progress).

Five old prints of the Abbey church of Cluny, ibid., 1928, p. 401.

CRANAGE, D. H. S. *The Home of the Monk*. Cambridge, 1926.

CUCHERAT, F. *Cluny au onzième siècle; son influence religieuse, intellectuelle et politique*. Lyon and Paris, 1881.

DAVID, DOM L. *Les grandes Abbayes de l'Occident*. Lille, 1907.

DEMIMUID, M. *Pierre le Vénérable, ou la vie et l'influence monastique au 12ᵉ siècle*, 1876.

DENIS, DOM P. Quelques notes sur les derniers moines de Cluny, in *Millénaire*, ii. 147.

DUPARAY, B. Pierre le Vénérable, Abbé de Cluny, in *Mémoires de la Société d'Histoire et d'Archéologie de Chalon-sur-Saône*, iv, 1858–62, Chalon-sur-Saône, p. 203.

Étude sur les mœurs des moines de Cluny au xiiᵉ siècle, in *Revue du Lyonnais*, 3rd series, xvii, 1858, p. 199.

GASTOUÉ, A. *L'Art Grégorien*. Paris, 1911.

GRAHAM, R. *English Ecclesiastical Studies*. London, 1928.

The Relation of Cluny to some other movements of monastic reform, in *Journal of Theological Studies*, 1913–14, xv. 179.

GREEVEN, N. *Die Wirksamkeit der Cluniacenser*. Wesel, 1870.

GUÉPRATTE. La Paix de Dieu, in *Mémoires de l'Académie de Metz*, 1856, p. 300.

GUILLOREAU, DOM L. Les prieurés anglais de l'Ordre de Cluny, in *Millénaire*, i. 291.

HEIMBUCHER, M. *Die Orden und Kongregationen der Katholischen Kirche*, (2nd. ed.). Paderborn 1907.

HELYOT, P., and BULLOT, M. *Histoire des ordres religieux*, Paris, 1792, vol. v.

HESSEL, A. Cluny und Mâcon, ein Beitrag zur Geschichte der päpstlichen Exemption-privilegien, in *Zeitschrift für Kirchengeschichte*, xxii, 1901, p. 516.

Odo von Cluni und das französische Kulturproblem im früheren Mittelalter, in *Hist. Zeitschrift*, cxxviii, 1923, p. 1.

JARDET, P. *Saint Odilon, Abbé de Cluny. Sa vie, son temps, ses œuvres*. Lyon, 1898.

KOLMER, L. *Odo, der erste Cluniacenser Magister*. Deggendorf, 1913.

LAFAY, G. Le Monnayage de Cluny, in *Millénaire*, ii. 325.

LASTEYRIE, C. DE. *L'Abbaye de Saint-Martial-de-Limoges*. Paris, 1901.

LEHMANN, R. *Forschungen zur Geschichte des Abtes Hugo I von Cluny*. Göttingen, 1869.

LETONNELIER, G. *L'Abbaye exempte de Cluny et le Saint-Siège*. *Archives de la France Monastique*, xxii. Ligugé and Paris, 1923.

LEX, L. Les peintures murales de la chapelle du Château des Moines de Cluny à Berzé-la-ville, in *Millénaire*, ii. 248.

L'HUILLIER, DOM A. *Vie de Saint Hugues, Abbé de Cluny, 1024–1109*. Solesmes, 1888.

LONGUEVAL, J. *Histoire de l'Église Gallicane*, viii, Paris, 1734, p. 228.

LORAIN, M. P. *Essai historique sur l'abbaye de Cluny.* Dijon, 1839.

LUCHAIRE, A. Cluni, in Lavisse, *Histoire de la France*, Paris, 1911, ii, pt. 2, p. 123.

MÂLE, E. *L'Art religieux du xii* siècle en France.* Paris, 1922.

MALINOWSKI, J. Étude historique sur Cluny, in *Revue du Lyonnais*, 3rd series, xvi. Lyon, 1873.

MONTALEMBERT, CTE. DE. *The Monks of the West, from St. Benedict to St. Bernard*, with an introduction by the Rev. F. A. Gasquet. London, 1896, vols. i, v, vi.

MORTET, V. Note sur la date de rédaction des coutumes de Cluny dites de Farfa, in *Millénaire*, i. 142.

NAEF, A. Les dates de construction de l'église de Romainmôtier, in *Bulletin Monumental*, lxx, 1906, p. 425.

OGERDIAS, L. J. *Histoire de Saint Mayol Abbé de Cluny.* Moulins, 1877.

OMONT, H. Manuscrit de Raban Maur offert par Saint Maieul à l'abbaye de Cluny, in *Millénaire*, i. 127.

PELARGUS, C. *Geschichte der Abtei Cluny.* Tübingen, 1858.

PENJON, A. *Cluny, la ville et l'abbaye.* Cluny, 1872. (2nd edition) 1884.

PETIT, E. Croisades bourguignonnes contre les Sarrazins d'Espagne au xiᵉ siècle, in *Revue Historique*, xxx, 1886, p. 259.

PFISTER, C. *Études sur le règne de Robert le Pieux, 996–1031.* Paris, 1885.

PIGNOT, J. H. *Histoire de l'Ordre de Cluny depuis la fondation jusqu'à la mort de Pierre le Vénérable.* Autun and Paris, 1868. 3 vols.

PLANCHER, U. *Histoire générale et particulière de la Bourgogne.* Dijon, 1739, 1741, 1748, and 1781.

POEY D'AVANT. *Monnaies féodales de France*, 1862, iii, p. 178.

POUZET, DR. Notes sur les chapiteaux de l'abbaye de Cluny, in *Revue de l'art chrétien*, lxii, 1912, pp. 1, 104.

RABY, F. J. E. *A History of Christian-Latin Poetry from the beginnings to the close of the Middle Ages.* Oxford, 1927.

RINGHOLZ, DOM O. Odilon von Cluny, in *Studien und Mitteilungen aus dem Ben. und Cisterc. Orden*, vol. i. 1–36, 289–313; ii. 1–27, 279–372. 1884.

— *Der Heilige Abt Odilo in seinem Leben und Werken.* Brünn, 1885.

ROY, L. A. *L'Abbaye de Baume-les-Messieurs.* Baume-les-Messieurs, 1892.

SACKUR, E. *Die Cluniacenser in ihrer kirchlichen und allgemeingeschichtlichen Wirksamkeit bis zur mitte des elften Jahrhunderts.* Halle, 1892. 2 vols.

— Handschriftliches aus Frankreich, in *Neues Archiv*, xv, 1890, p. 105.

SAINT MAUR, CONGRÉGATION DE. *Histoire Littéraire de la France . . . par des Religieux Bénédictins de la Congrégation de Saint Maur*, vol. vii, Paris, 1746, pp. 399 and 414; vol. viii, 1747, p. 390; and vol. ix, 1750, p. 465.

SANDYS, J. E. *A History of Classical Scholarship*, vol. i. Cambridge, 1921. (3rd edition.)

SCHEUTEN, P. *Das Mönchtum in der altfranzösischen Profandichtung (12–14. Jahrhundert).* Münster in Westf., 1919.

SCHUSTER, DOM H. De fastorum agiographico ordine imperialis monasterii pharphensis, in *Millénaire*, i. 146.

SMITH, L. M. Cluny and Gregory VII, in *English Historical Review*, xxvi, 1911, p. 20.

The Early History of the Monastery of Cluny. Oxford, 1920.

TERRET, ABBÉ V. *La Sculpture bourguignonne au XIIe et XIIIe siècles; ses origines et ses sources d'inspiration; Cluny*. Autun, 1914.

THOMASSIN. *Ancienne et nouvelle discipline de l'Eglise*. Paris, 1678. 3 vols.

THOMPSON, J. W. On the identity of Bernard of Cluny, in *Journal of Theological Studies*, viii, 1906-7, p. 394.

VALOIS, J. DE. Sur quelques points d'histoire relatifs à la fondation de Cluny, in *Millénaire*, i. 177.

VALOUS, G. DE. *Le domaine de l'abbaye de Cluny aux Xe et XIe siècles.* Paris, 1923: and in *Annales de l'académie de Mâcon*, 3rd series, xxii, Mâcon, 1920-I, p. 285.

VAQUIER, A. Une réforme de Cluny en 1428, in *Revue Bénédictine*, xxxvi. 159.

VERDIER, A. *Album de Cluny*, 1852. No. 8 of *Catalogue de la Bibliothèque de la Commission des Monuments Historiques*. Paris, 1875.

VIREY, J. *L'Abbaye de Cluny*. (Petites Monographies des Grands Edifices de la France.) Paris, 1927.

Un ancien plan de l'abbaye de Cluny, in *Millénaire*, ii. 231.

L'Architecture romane dans l'ancien diocèse de Mâcon. Paris, 1892.

WILMART, DOM A. Le couvent et la bibliothèque de Cluny vers le milieu du onzième siècle, in *Revue Mabillon*, xi, Paris and Ligugé, 1921, p. 89.

Cluny, manuscrits liturgiques de, in Dom F. Cabrol and Dom H. Leclercq, *Dictionnaire d'archéologie chrétienne*, iii, Paris, 1914, part 2, col. 2074.

Gallia Christiana vetus, 1656, iv. 271, 966; nova, 1728, iv. 1117.

ADDITIONAL BIBLIOGRAPHY

AUBERT, M. 'Les plus anciens croisés d'ogives'. (*Bull. Mon.*, XCIII, 5, 137, 1934).

'Cluny'. (*Cong. Arch.*, XCVIII, 503, (1935)).

CHAGNY, A. *Cluny et son empire*. Paris, London, Ryvust, (after 1931).

CONANT, KENNETH JOHN. 'The Apse at Cluny'. (*Speculum*, VII,1, 23-35, Jan. 1932).

'Cluny: les églises et la maison du Chef d'Ordre'. (*Spec. Med. Acad. Am.*, Mâcon, Protat Frères). In the press.

With R. W. LLOYD. 'Cluny epigraphy'. (*Spec.* VII,3, 336-349, July 1932).

'The Date of the ambulatory capitals'. (*Spec.*, V,1, 77-94, Jan. 1931).

'Les dimensions systématiques et symboliques à l'Eglise abbatiale de Cluny'. (*Ann. Acad. Mâcon,* 3rd series, XLV, 2-5, 1960-61, Mâcon, 1962).

'Drawings and photographs of the transept'. (*Spec.,* IV,3, 291-294, July 1929).

'El monasterio de Cluny en Borgona'. (*An Inst. Arte Am. Invest. Est.,* V, 9-20, 1952. Univ. Buenos Aires).

'Final stages of the project'. (*Spec.,* XXIX,1, 1-43, Jan. 1954).

'Five old prints of the abbey church of Cluny'. (*Spec.,* III,3, 401-404, July 1928).

'The Iconography and sequence of the ambulatory capitals of Cluny.' (*Spec.,* V,3, 378-387, July 1930).

'Measurements and proportions of the great church at Cluny'. (*Atken z. VIII Kongr. f. Frühmittelaltenforschung,* 21-28, Sept. 1958, 230-238, Graz, 1962).

'Preliminary restoration drawings of the Abbey Church'. (*Spec.,* IV,2, 168-170, April 1929).

'Les rapports architectureaux entre Cluny et Payerne'. (*Biblio. Hist. Vaud.,* XXXIX, 127-138, Lausanne, 1966).

'The Season of 1928'. (*Spec.,* IV,1, 3-26, Jan. 1931).

'The Season of 1929'. (*Spec.,* VI,1, 3-14, Jan. 1931).

'The Significance of the Abbey Church'. (*Spec.,* IV,3, 291-294, Oct. 1929).

'Systematic dimensions in the buildings'. (*Spec.,* XXVIII,1, 1-45, Jan. 1963).

'The third church at Cluny'. (*Med. St.,* II, 327-338, Harvard Univ. Pr., 1939).

'Two new books about Cluny'. (*Spec.,* XVII, 4, 563-565, Oct. 1942).

DICKSON, M. and C. *Les églises romanes de l'ancien diocèse de Chalon.* Mâcon, 1935.

EVANS, JOAN. *Cluniac art of the romanesque period.* Cambridge, 1938. *Romanesque architecture of the order of Cluny.* Cambridge, 1950.

FOCILLON, H. *Peintures romanes des églises de France.* Paris, 1938

GRAHAM, R. and CLAPHAM, A. W. 'The Monastery of Cluny, 910-1155'. (*Archaeologia,* LXXX, 143, Oxford, 1930).

MERCIER, F. *Les primitifs français: la peinture clunysienne en Bourgogne à l'époque romane.* Paris, n.d. (1931).

REUTTER, E. *Les représentations de la musique dans la sculpture romane en France.* Paris, 1938.

TALOBRE, J. 'La reconstitution du portail de d'église abbatiale de Cluny'. (*Bull. Mon,* CII, 225, (1944)).

VIREY, J. *Les églises romanes de l'ancien diocèse de Mâcon.* 2nd ed., Mâcon, 1935.

THE ABBOTS OF CLUNY
910–1157

(Dijon, MS. fonds Baudot, 1018, p. 114. Dates there missing or incorrect added in brackets.)

910 Saint Berno de Bourgogne.
[926] Saint Odo de Dôle.
[944] Saint Aymard d'Angoulême.
[954] Saint Mayeul de Forcalquier.
[994] Saint Odile de Mercœur.
[1049] Saint Hugues de Semur-en-Brionnais.
[1109] Pons de Melgueil.
[1122] Hugues II de Semur.
[1122] Pierre de Montboissier (le Vénérable).
[1157] Hugues III de Montlhéry.

I
THE FOUNDATION OF THE ABBEY OF CLUNY

IN the year 909 two friends set out together from Tours. The time had not yet come when men went out as knights, in search of adventure; these two rode forth as men of religion in search of monastic virtue.[1] The one, Odo, a man of thirty, had from his infancy been dedicated to monastic life: when he was a baby his father had vowed him to St. Martin; and when he was a boy, by temperament and physique unfitted for feudal life, his father had had to admit the force of the vow and to send his son to receive the tonsure and to become a canon of St. Martin at Tours. There he had turned to a life of scholarship and piety; and thence had gone for a time to Paris for further study. Adhegrin, his friend, was of another stamp. He had lived longer in the world, until he wearied of feudal life[2] and took refuge at St. Martin's. Yet even there neither had found the peace he sought; discipline was lax, religion conventional, and the canons for the most part self-seeking and unworthy of their respect. So finally they determined to set out in search of a monastery where religious fervour still glowed, where the Benedictine vows of poverty, chastity, and obedience were still kept, and the claustral virtues of be-nignity, simplicity, and cheerfulness were still cherished. Over the wide plains of the Loire, up hill and down dale, into the forests of the Morvan, they rode in search of their ideal; but nowhere was it to be found. At last Odo turned back in discouragement to a hermit's cell near Tours; but Adhegrin went forward with the hope of reaching Rome, until the track seemed to come to an end in a strange valley of the Jura, where towering vertical cliffs of pale rock hemmed in a green valley that lay like a lake at their feet. There his quest ended; for in that place he found the monastery of Baume[3] which in its solitude had kept the

---

[1] John of Salerno, *Vita Odonis*; Marrier, 23.
[2] He was attached to the court of Fulk of Anjou.
[3] Now Baume-les-Messieurs. For its history see Sackur, i. 37.

Benedictine ideal of peace and order undefiled. Rejoicing, Adhegrin was received into its community; and at his urgent summons Odo once more left his cell at Tours, and set out, bearing with him his library of a hundred books, to join his friend.

At Baume the discipline was severe and the rule of Benedict of Aniane was strictly followed. Certain hours of silence were always kept, and during the penitential seasons no one was allowed to speak except in chapter; in Advent and Holy Week deep silence was kept day and night.[1] The Abbot had more despotic power even than was customary in other houses; and the monks had to follow an exaggerated ideal of humility. Adhegrin could bear ascetic privation, but not a common life or strict authority. After little more than a year he retired to live as a hermit in a wooded gorge near the abbey. There he lived on beans and wild berries, with no other company than the birds and beasts; 'patitur nimirum omni tempore frigus, et calorem: calorem inter scapulas, frigus inter manus et brachia'.[2] Even thus he had no spiritual peace, and passed years in torment and temptations in which visions of St. Martin were his only strength and consolation.[3]

Odo, however, was born for the cloister; and the seal was put on his monastic task by his ordination as a priest[4] and by his appointment to the charge of the oblates of the abbey. After a time he returned to Touraine to persuade his parents to follow him into the cloister; his mother entered a nunnery, and his father followed him back to Baume.[5]

Berno, their Abbot, was a noble Burgundian, nephew of Lewis the Stammerer. Drawn to religion from his youth, he had early renounced the world, and founded a monastery, of which he later became Abbot, at his own home at Gigny.

[1] John of Salerno, op. cit.; Marrier, 27.
[2] Ibid.; Marrier, 25.
[3] At his death he was buried in the abbey; his bones still rest in their reliquaries upon the high altar.
[4] Only a certain number of monks in each monastery were ordained to celebrate the necessary sacraments for their brethren. John of Salerno tells an odd monkish tale of the Bishop of Limoges, Turpion d'Aubusson, who ordained Odo: 'De quo videlicet episcopo narrare solet pater Odo, quia benedictum ab eo cibum nullus canis audebat comedere. Quod si casu contigisset, mox canis ille moriebatur, veluti pro cibo aliquid gustasset venenatum' (Marrier, 30).
[5] Pignot, i. 93.

He brought into the cloister the qualities that would have
served him at court: a power of judging character, a
capacity for administration, courteous manners, and a steadfast will. To govern was natural to him; and when he undertook to restore the abbey of Baume, seven leagues from
Gigny, after its devastation by the Normans, he continued
to rule Gigny also.[1] Such responsibilities kept him in touch
with a greater world than that of the cloister. Rudolf, King
of Transjuran Burgundy, had to be persuaded to confirm
the affiliation of Baume to Gigny; and Berno had to go to
Rome to obtain from Pope Formosus a deed infeodating
Gigny to St. Peter, and an Act of immunity for both
monasteries from all tithes and authorities but that of the
Holy See.

In the summer of 910,[2] a year after Odo and Adhegrin had
entered Baume, Berno found himself summoned to the
Mâconnais on another errand: one that was to cause his
name to be remembered through the centuries to come.
William Duke of Aquitaine, Marquis of Gothia, Count of
Auvergne, Velay, and Bourges, had reached old age and
found himself without an heir. His only son was dead; his
nephew had no children. There was thus a term fixed to his
enjoyment of his worldly goods; and his conscience was
haunted by the memory of a murder committed in a fit of
passion. Therefore he was inclined to generosity, and
wished to make reparation for his sins by founding a
monastery. To this end he summoned Berno, who came in
company of Hugh, Abbot of the monastery of St. Martin at
Autun. The question of site was the first to be decided, and
Berno fixed upon some land at Cluny which William of
Aquitaine had received from his sister Ava when she took
monastic vows.[3] It was a wide valley, sheltered by wooded
hills that shut it off cloister-wise from the highway of the

[1] Anonymous Life of Odo, B.N. 5566, fol. 21, discovered by Sackur (Sackur, i. 38;
L. M. Smith, p. 10). The other account of his life that makes him a monk of Saint-
Savin near Poitiers, sent with seventeen others to restore the abbey of St. Martin at
Autun, and thence sent to reform Baume, seems less worthy of credence, since in
later history Baume was dependent on Gigny (ibid., p. 11). On the life of Berno see
J. de Valois, 'Sur quelques points d'histoire relatifs à la fondation de Cluny,' in
Millénaire de Cluny, i, p. 196.

[2] Pignot dates the foundation of Cluny to 909 (i. 16), but the accepted year is 910
(Sackur, i. 40). It was in the eleventh year of Charles the Simple.

[3] For its history see J. de Valois, p. 196.

Saône—a site and a position that may well have commended itself to Berno from its likeness to his own home and abbey of Gigny. William of Aquitaine held other views; he objected that Cluny was the best hunting-ground in all his domains. 'Drive your hounds hence', said Berno, 'and put monks in their places; for you know which will serve you better before God, the baying of hounds or the prayers of monks': and William, with murder upon his conscience, could only agree.

In the early autumn William of Aquitaine went to Bourges, one of his chief cities, to hold his seigneurial assize. There on 11 September, in the presence of his wife, his nephews, Odo Count of Toulouse, Gontard of Poitiers, Gerald of Aurillac, Adhemar of Bourbon and other lords, Adalard Bishop of Clermont, and Madalbert, patriarch of Aquitaine, he signed the charter that was to give the abbey of Cluny its existence, its independence, and its power.

'To those who consider things sanely it is evident that Divine Providence counsels the rich to use well those goods that they possess in transitory fashion, if they wish for eternal recompense. And Holy Writ shows this to be possible, for such counsel is manifest in the saying: "the ransom of a man's life is his riches." [1] Wherefore I, William, by the grace of God count and duke, having pondered these things and wishing while there is yet time to make provision for my salvation, have found it right, yea necessary, to dispose for the good of my soul of some of the temporal possessions which have been bestowed upon me. For since I appear to have increased them much, I would not wish to deserve the reproach in the hour of death that I had used them only for the needs of my body, but would rather, when my last moment shall take them all from me, give myself the joy of having used a part for my soul: the which may not be better done than by following the precept of our Lord: "I will make myself friends among the poor". That this benefaction may endure not only for a time, but may last for ever, I will provide at my expense for men living together under monastic vows, with this faith and hope that if I cannot myself despise all the things of this world, at least by sustaining those who despise the world, those whom I believe to be righteous in the eyes of God, I may myself receive the reward of the righteous.

'To all those who live in the unity of faith and who implore the

[1] Prov. xiii. 8.

mercy of Christ, to all who shall succeed them and shall be living
so long as the world endures, I make known that for the love of
God and of our Saviour Christ Jesus I give and deliver to the
Apostles Peter and Paul the village [1] of Cluny, on the river Grosne,
with its curtilage [2] and its house, [3] with the Chapel that is dedicated
in honour of St. Mary Mother of God and of St. Peter, Prince of
the Apostles, with all the property that depends thereon, cottages, [4]
chapels, serfs both men and women, vines, fields, meadows, forests,
water and watercourses, mills, crops and revenues, land tilled
and untilled, with no reservations. All these things are situate in
the county of Mâcon or near it, each enclosed within its bounds.
I, William, with my wife Ingelberge, give these things to the
aforesaid Apostles, first for the love of God, then for the soul of
my lord the King Eudes, for the souls of my father and mother,
for me and my wife, that is for the salvation of our souls and
bodies, for the soul of Ava my sister who left me these properties
by will, for the souls of our brothers and sisters, our nephews and
of all our kindred, men and women, for our faithful servants, and
for the maintenance and integrity of the Catholic faith. Finally,
since as Christians we are all bound together by the bonds of our
faith and charity, may this gift be made also for the faithful of
times past, present and to come.

'I give on condition that a Regular Monastery be established at
Cluny in honour of the apostles Peter and Paul; that monks shall
form a congregation there living under the rule of St. Benedict;
that they shall for ever possess, hold and order the property given
in such wise that this honourable house shall be unceasingly full
of vows and prayers, that men shall seek there with a lively desire
and an inner fervour the sweetness of converse with Heaven, and
that prayers and supplications shall be addressed thence without
ceasing to God, both for me and for those persons commemorated
above.

'We ordain also that our foundation shall serve for ever as
a refuge for those who having renounced the world as poor men
bring nothing with them but their good will, and we desire that
our superfluity shall become their abundance. May the monks and
all the aforesaid possessions be under the power and dominion of
Abbot Berno, who shall rule according to his knowledge and

---

[1] *Villa*—once an agrarian unit, it had become a simple geographical term more or
less equivalent to our 'village'. On these terms see G. de Valous, pp. 351, 355, 358.
[2] *Curtilus*—an estate, generally including vineyard, meadow, and wood, with rights
of wood-cutting and water; but sometimes rather vaguely used.
[3] *Mansus indominicatus*—a freehold house with land attached and generally with
a family of serfs established there.
[4] *Colonia*—the residence of a serf and his family, sometimes with land attached.

power so long as he shall live. After his death may the monks have the power and liberty to elect as abbot and ruler the monk of their order whom they shall prefer, according to the good pleasure of God and the rule laid down by St. Benedict, with no contradiction or impediment of this election by our power or that of any man. Nevertheless every five years they shall pay to Rome twelve pieces of gold for the upkeep of the candles of the Church of the Apostles. May they have as protectors the Apostles themselves, and for defender the Pontiff of Rome. Out of the fullness of their hearts and souls may they themselves build a monastery in this place, according to their knowledge and capacity. We also desire that in our time and in the time of our successors, as much at least as the circumstances of the time and the situation of the place admit, they may each day perform with fervent zeal works of mercy to the poor, to beggars, strangers and travellers.

'It has pleased us to set forth in this testament that from this day forward the monks united in congregation at Cluny shall be wholly freed from our power, from that of our kindred, and from the jurisdiction of royal greatness, and shall never submit to the yoke of any earthly power. I beg and pray that no secular Prince, no Count, no Bishop, no Pontiff of the Roman Church, by God and through God and all his saints, under threat of the awful day of judgement, may ever invade the possessions of these servants of God. Let him not sell, nor diminish, nor exchange, nor take any thing which is theirs; let him set up no ruler over them against their will. That this prohibition may bind the bold and evil with straiter bonds, once again I say it, and add: I conjure you, ye Holy Apostles and glorious Princes of the Earth, Peter and Paul; and thou, Pontiff of Pontiffs of the Apostolic See, do ye cut off from the communion of the Holy Catholic Church and from life eternal, by the canonical and apostolic authority received from God, those who steal, invade or sell these things which I give to you with eager wish and a joyful heart. Be ye the guardians and defenders of Cluny and of the servants of God who shall dwell there, and of their goods that are destined for the giving of alms, for the imitation of the lovingkindness and mercy of our most Holy Redeemer . . .'

The charter ends with a terrible curse on any man who should attempt to upset it or to violate its provisions. William of Aquitaine himself went to Rome to ratify the donation, to infeodate the monastery to the Holy See, and to pay to John X the first of the promised dues.[1]

[1] Pignot, i. 34.

Thus Berno was consecrated Abbot of Cluny by Gideon, Archbishop of Besançon. He was accompanied to Cluny according to Benedictine custom by twelve monks, drawn from his monasteries of Gigny and Baume, who were to form the nucleus of the new community. The monastery was rather poorly endowed,[1] but all that was needed for building was close at hand: forests of ancient trees, and quarries of red and grey stone. Before five years were out a primitive chapel had been built, dedicated to St. Peter and St. Paul, and some rude accommodation for the small community had been constructed or adapted to their use.

There was little to differentiate Cluny from hundreds of other Benedictine monasteries in France, or to indicate the greatness of its destinies. It was poor; it had no ancient history. It lay on no great route of trade or pilgrimage. But though, as one of its monks said,[2] 'it was a valley shut off, far from all human contact, which breathed such a perfume of aloofness, repose, and peace, that it seemed like a heavenly solitude', it was not far from such centres as Mâcon, Tournus, Chalon-sur-Saône, and Autun, and easily achieved contact with a world outside its own cloister.[3] The district, too, was rich in monastic associations, for since no serious barbarian invasion had ever crossed the hills between the Nivernais and the Morvan to the north, and the Mâconnais and the Charollais to the south, monastic communities from other parts of France had taken refuge there from the Normans: monks from Fleury at Perrecy, from Noirmoutiers and Saint-Florent at Tournus. Moreover, the land was free from the dominion of any overlord: as Peter the Venerable was later to remind the Pope, 'sine rege et principe existens'[4]; and by its foundation charter it was made directly dependent upon the Papacy and subject to no other dominion or authority.[5] Thus, since they owed homage

---

[1] Radulphus Glaber, Bk. III, cap. 5. 'Quod etiam Coenobium in primo, non amplius quam quindecim terrae colonias dicitur in dotem accepisse, fratres tamen duodecim numero ibi memorantur convenisse.'   [2] Quoted Pignot, i. 30.

[3] Pignot points out (i. 31) that a branch of Agrippa's great road from Lyons to Boulogne by Mâcon, Autun, and Avallon started from Belleville and went by Avenas, Ouroux, Brandon, Clermain, and Sainte-Cécile up the valley of the Grosne itself, to rejoin the main road at Autun.   [4] *Epist.* Lib. i. 21 (Marrier, 649) to Innocent II.

[5] For a full bibliography of original sources on the legal position of the abbey and a careful study of its 'exempted' position see G. Letonnelier, 'L'Abbaye exempte de Cluny et le Saint-Siège', in *Archives de la France monastique*, xxii.

neither to Emperor nor King nor to any great local lord, Cluny and its land were fitted to become the seat of a monastic kingdom exempt from civil powers.

The last safeguard of the liberty of Cluny, established by its charter, was that of the free election of its Abbot by the monks. Berno, however, wished to impose his will upon his brethren even after death. When he died in 926 [1] he disposed by testament of the abbacies of Gigny, Baume, and Cluny, as well as of the lesser houses of which he had become Abbot, as if they had been his private property.

He designated Wido, his nephew, as Abbot of the monasteries of Gigny and Mouthier-en-Bresse and of the cell of Saint-Lauthien; and to Cluny, Massay, and Déols he appointed Odo.[2] He further directed that La Frette, an ancient priory of Baume, together with its village and its lands, and a quarter of the salt-mines of Lons-le-Saunier were to go to the abbey of Cluny, which was to pay an annual due of twelve deniers to Gigny. Berno was conscious that such a bequest might be criticized; his testament continues:

'Let this not seem an injustice, if I have assigned these properties to Cluny, for it is there that I have chosen the place of my burial; for it is as it were orphaned by the death of my lord William, the illustrious duke, and will remain unfinished in consequence of my own. Moreover it is the poorest in possessions and yet has the greatest number of monks; wherefore, if it has pleased the divine bounty to grant me after my first children and my first home a new home and yet more children, it appears to me just to let them have a share of my heritage; for though they live in a different monastery, they are none the less bound to the service of the same master, the blessed Peter, in whose name I have built both my monasteries.'

Naturally Wido, who was already Abbot of Baume, disputed the provision of Berno's will; but Odo appealed to Rome, and the Pope—perhaps more inclined to equity than justice, perhaps respecting the strength of Berno's character in death as in life—gave his decision in favour of Cluny.

So Odo, who had been consecrated Abbot immediately

---

[1] William of Aquitaine had died in 918.
[2] The will of Berno is printed in Marrier, 9. On Déols see Sackur, i. 63. It did not remain permanently attached to Cluny. On Massay see ibid., i. 64.

after Berno's death, left Baume for Cluny, and took up the government of its abbey. He made a tomb for Berno behind the altar of St. Benedict in the abbey church,[1] and endeavoured faithfully to carry out the provisions of Berno's will. For in his testament the old Abbot had not merely decided the fate of his abbeys, but had endeavoured to guide their conduct:

'Wherefore, O abbots and brethren here present, and ye who shall come in the future, I conjure you in the name of the mercy of the God in whose sight we live, to keep staunchly united, to observe with the same exactness as before the established usage in chanting the psalms, in keeping silence, in the quality of food and raiment, and above all in the contempning of personal property. If any man should contumaciously allow any of these precepts to lapse, by the authority of the Holy Rule I enjoin the Abbots of the two monasteries to lend each other their mutual support to correct their erring brother. If any man should think to infringe the present constitution in any particular, may he be turned aside from his purpose by this threat from God: "Cursed be he that removeth his neighbour's landmark"—that is, he who breaks down what has been set up by an act of the Divine Will. . . .'

The maintenance of the Benedictine rule in its integrity became, indeed, the main task of Odo, who brought to his work the enthusiasm of a man who had found in that rule a perfect way of life. He thus unconsciously laid the foundation of the future greatness of Cluny; for it was as a centre of Benedictine orthodoxy that the abbey was to gain influence, riches and power.[2] Radulphus Glaber traces the descent of the true Benedictine tradition from Glanfeuil to Saint-Savin, thence to Saint-Martin-d'Autun and thence to Baume: 'till finally, as it were wearied of this long pilgrimage, God willed that it should choose for resting-place and for its throne of wisdom the monastery of Cluny, where the seed that it bore was soon to prove infinitely fruitful.'[3]

[1] The precursor of Saint-Pierre-le-Vieux, built by Maiol.
[2] Cf. Pet. Ven., *Epist.*, vi. 17 to priors and sub-priors of Cluniac houses: 'Odo, inquam, primus Cluniacensis Ordinis Pater, qui emortuum iam, et pene ubique sepultum monastici propositi feruorem ressuscitare suo conamine agressus est. Defecerat suo tempore Sanctus: diminutae erant veritates a filiis hominum. In cunctis pene Europae nostrae finibus, de Monacho, praeter tonsuram et habitum, nihil. Instituit ille divino operi fere tunc solus, et Cluniaci prima iaciens fundamenta, post, huc illucque Religionis semina, quandiu advixit, serere non cessavit.' Marrier, 58.
[3] Radulphus Glaber, *Historiarum libri V*, Lib. III, cap. v.

II

THE GROWTH OF THE CLUNIAC ORDER

THE monasteries of western Europe had not yet recovered from the ravages of the Normans and Hungarians, and in the strict Benedictine rule many men saw a hope of re-establishing their solidarity. Consequently Odo was soon called away from Cluny to establish the rule he practised in other houses: first in the monastery of Saint-Géraud-d'Aurillac,[1] then at its dependent foundation of Saint-Pons-de Thomières[2]; then in 936 he was summoned by the Pope to Rome and given the task of reforming various Roman monasteries of which the greatest was the ancient abbey of St. Paul without the walls.[3] On his return to France he helped to revive the monasteries of Saint-Austremoine at Clermont,[4] Saint-Pierre-le-Vif at Sens,[5] Saint-Martin at Tulle,[6] Saint-Pierre at Lézat,[7] Saint-Sauveur at Sarlat,[8] Saint-Martial at Limoges,[9] Saint-Sore-de-Genouillac,[10] and Saint-Benoît at Fleury.[11] Then in 939 Hugh of Italy gave him control of San Pietro al Ciel d'Oro at Pavia[12]; and finally he undertook the reform of Saint-Julien at Tours,[13] in collaboration with his old friend Theotolon, who had been a canon with him at Saint Martin's some twenty years before. As John of Salerno records:[14] 'Postmodum vero abbas ordinatus, Franciarum, Aquitaniarum, Hispaniarumque partium, atque Romanae urbis circumstantium Coenobiorum, effectus est dux et pater dulcissimus.'

Such reforms, however much they increased the influence of Cluny, did nothing to add to its temporal greatness. The

[1] Pignot, i. 147; Sackur, i. 77.   [2] Sackur, i. 86.
[3] Marrier, 25; Sackur, i. 101.
[4] Pignot, i. 164; Sackur, i. 85. By 937 it was independent of Cluny.
[5] Pignot, i. 165; Sackur, i. 92.
[6] Sackur, i. 78. Odo was invited to become abbot, but refused; another Cluniac monk was elected. The abbey retained its independence.
[7] Sackur, i. 80.   [8] Pignot, i. 164; Sackur, i. 80.
[9] Sackur, i. 81. In February 942 Odo (as abbot of Fleury) and the abbots of Saint-Martial and Solignac made a pact together to be governed by one rule and to be considered one community.   [10] Sackur, i. 80.
[11] Pignot, i. 156. Other reforms associated with Odo's influence are enumerated in Sackur, i. 82 et seqq.   [12] Pignot, i. 176.
[13] Pignot, i. 166; Sackur, i. 92.   [14] Marrier, 15.

monasteries revived and restored by Odo retained their autonomy—an autonomy that itself formed a part of the Benedictine tradition—and however close at the time was their connexion with Cluny, there was no question of real affiliation. At Fleury, indeed, to which Odo had been summoned by Hugh, Duke of the Franks, the monks first resisted his entry by force and then sent a deputation to show him their charters of independence. At length they consented to receive him on condition that he entered the monastery alone, riding upon an ass in token of humility.[1] Even the Charter granted by John XI in 931,[2] that gave to Cluny the right to receive into the community monks from other monasteries that had fallen into decay, until such time as their original houses should be reformed, swelled the numbers of the abbey but not its revenues.

Yet at the same time Cluny was slowly increasing its worldly wealth through the donations of the faithful. In 921, while Berno still reigned, Adhemar, count of Matric-sur-Eure, gave to Cluny the 'cour' of Souvigny and its church of St. Peter, together with the adjacent houses and fields, the water-meadows in the valley, the vineyards on the hillside, the forests on the hills, and the junipers that grew at their edge.[3] His desire, however, was less to benefit the monks than to form an inhabited centre to his domain; and when the twelve monks of Cluny that migrated thither to found the new monastery proved successful in their agricultural enterprises he wished to take back some of the land. But he soon repented, and in 926 had a testament drawn up by which he bequeathed them more land and annexed to them the oratory of Sainte-Marie at Moulins, to found an anniversary for himself and his kin, and to secure for himself and his family the privilege of burial in the abbey.[4] Adhemar left his lands 'to Cluny or to Souvigny': the future was as yet uncertain and the relation of Souvigny to Cluny not quite clear.

After the ratification of Berno's will and the installation of Odo as Abbot, the temporal position of Cluny was still far from being assured. The abbey buildings were unfinished

---

[1] Pignot, i. 156. [2] Migne, *Pat. Lat.*, cxxxii. 1055.
[3] Pignot, i. 45. Souvigny, perhaps because it was too near to Cluny, never acquired great estates. [4] Pignot, i. 47.

and its endowment was inadequate. Saint Martin came to Odo in a vision and promised him great riches out of Gothia and Aquitaine; but it was only gradually that the promise was fulfilled. Such gifts as the abbey had received from the great had not so far profited it much. In 927 Acfred, the nephew of William of Aquitaine, had given to Cluny the church that his uncle had built at Sauxillange and the lands with which he had generously endowed it; but it was some years before a priory could be established there.[1] Two years later Adelaide, wife of the Duke of Burgundy, gave to Cluny the ancient Juran monastery of Romainmôtier on condition that the two abbeys should form a single congregation under one Abbot; but it was more than fifty years before Cluny entered into effectual possession of the gift.[2] Similarly, Cluny did not enter into possession of the abbey of Charlieu, given to Odo by Hugh of Italy and Leo VII in 938, until 990.[3]

More profitable were small gifts of agricultural land that were offered to Cluny: at first in its immediate vicinity, then, under Odo, all over the counties of Mâcon, Lyons, Chalon, and Autun, and in the districts of La Bresse, of the Rhone and Provence.[4] Often the gift involved some return: the celebration of an anniversary, the upkeep of a lamp, or the burning of ten deniers' worth of wax candles on Saint Benedict's day,[5] or mention in the ordinary prayers. Already by the time of Odo an 'obituary', called the *martyrologium*, *Kalendarium*, or *liber vitae*, was drawn up, in which such benefactions and the prayers and offerings due in return were noted.[6]

Odo's relations with kings and courts secured the abbey two charters of importance. In 927 Rudolf of Burgundy, King of the Franks, gave Cluny a charter that confirmed its

---

[1] Pignot, i. 43, 198.
[2] On the history of Romainmôtier see Naef, and Sackur, i. 73.
[3] Boson, Duke of Provence, seized it; and though he left it to Cluny by his will it remained in the hands of other lords. Only at the Council of Anse in 990 did the Abbot of Cluny succeed in establishing his claim. Pignot, i. 413.
[4] Pignot, i. 212; de Valous, p. 325. Between 910 and 980 there were no less than 630 such gifts of land. To understand in how many small parcels of land from how many benefactors the abbey acquired its property, the reader is referred to Bernard and Bruel's six large volumes, and to the bibliography given in G. de Valous, p. 475.
[5] Ibid., p. 327.
[6] It was kept up until the seventeenth century; and is unhappily now lost (ibid., p. 326).

autonomy and granted the abbey the right of coining its own money[1]; and in 939 Louis d'Outremer gave the abbey a similar solemn confirmation, with a precise enumeration of its rights.

'Let them pay no market tolls; let no man trouble their freemen or their serfs; let them own as lords and by seigneurial title the tithes intended for the upkeep of their hostel for pilgrims and travellers; let them enjoy possession of their churches and of the tithes attached to them under the conditions on which they were acquired; let no man trouble them in the possession of their farms; let them claim of right the fields that belong to them and the allods that have been given them, in whatsoever country or parish they may lie; let no man, without their consent, collect the due of *terrage* on any forests or lands which they hold entire.'[2]

Even so, the position of the abbey remained somewhat precarious; and it may have been with the knowledge that Cluny needed an Abbot who would devote his capacities to Cluniac affairs rather than to Benedictine monasticism as a whole, that Odo in 938 appointed the monk Aymar as his coadjutor.[3] Six years later Odo died at Tours[4] in the sixty-fourth year of his age and the fifteenth of his rule, and Aymar was elected to rule in his stead.[5]

Aymar was a man altogether lacking in the great qualities that had made Odo the friend of Kings and Popes and one of the great churchmen of France; his chief virtue was his humility. Even his panegyrists could only call him simple and innocent. But under his rule the possessions of the abbey were increased and brought into better order.[6] Possession of the abbey lands at Souvigny, some of which

[1] Bruel, i. 285. The privilege was confirmed by Pope John XI in 931, and was exercised for some 300 years. The money of Cluny was of uniform type, stamped on the obverse with a cross and the legend CENOBIO CLVNIACO, and on the reverse with a key and the legend PETRVS ET PAVLVS. One *sou clunisois* was worth five *sous parisis*. See Barthélemy, p. 33. Souvigny later also acquired the right of coining money; William V of Aquitaine gave the abbey the mint of Niort about 1020, and his wife Agnes the mints of Saint-Jean-d'Angély and Mougon : Cucherat, p. 10 note.
[2] Marrier, 265.   [3] Bruel, i. 486.
[4] He was in Rome when he realized that he was dying, and made his way back to Tours, the home of his youth. He got there in time to celebrate four days of the Saint's festival, and died on 14 December 942 in church during the celebrations. He was buried in the crypt of Saint-Julien at Tours. Marrier, 55.
[5] Sackur, i. 205.
[6] Cf. Odilo on Aymar: 'Hic in augmentatione praediorum et adquisitione temporalis commodi adeo studiosus fuit.' Marrier, 269.

had been seized by Adhemar's nephew Aymon, was secured[1]; and the daughter house of Sauxillange received its definite organization and was established with twelve monks.[2] The priories of Saint-Jean and Saint-Martin at Mâcon were established.[3] At first Cluny had both rented land and leased it to others; but under Aymar the abbey began to find its own land sufficient and to exploit it more skilfully. In Cluny itself outlying parts were purchased to round off the whole,[4] and there and elsewhere exchanges were negotiated so that little by little a true 'estate' was created. The men to work it went with the land; each *mansus* had its family of serfs, sometimes two or three, sometimes as many as five[5]; and such serfs were the absolute property of the monastery. A crime committed against them was a crime against the monks; in 944, for example, a man named Richer, vassal of the Viscount of Vienne, killed a serf of Cluny named Egruinus, and in reparation, with the consent of his overlord, made himself the serf of the monastery in the stead of his victim. He made solemn declaration:

'I deliver my person and my head to the abbey of Cluny. The Abbot and the monks shall have the power to keep me in their hands, to exchange me, or to sell me. I consent that everything I may acquire in the future shall pass to the monastery absolutely. I give up the right of doing anything or going anywhere without their permission. Henceforward let them have the power to do what they will with me.'[6]

Land which was as yet undeveloped—especially land suited to vines—was sometimes brought into cultivation by leasing it to a peasant on the system of the *medium plantum* or *complant*: it was let out on condition that the tenant should build a cottage and plant vines within a certain time. When this

---

[1] Pignot, i. 233.   [2] Pignot, i. 198; Sackur, i. 208.
[3] *Bullarium Cluniacense*, 5; Sackur, i. 207.
[4] Valous points out that when a man gave 'villam cum omne sua integritate' it only meant what *he* held there, which might be, and often was, a very ragged parcel, p. 343. At Cluny—unlike Vézelay, Souvigny, La Charité, and Moissac—the relations between the townsfolk and the abbey were always friendly. A communal franchise was given by St. Hugh about 1090, and the town was surrounded by a wall with eight gates (of which two survive) about 1179. The abbey had its own walls and towers round its precincts, and five towers (mostly of the fourteenth and fifteenth centuries) survive.
[5] Ibid., p. 353. See also R. Houdayer, 'L'exploitation agricole des moines de Cluny', in *Millénaire de Cluny*, i, p. 235.
[6] *Chartes et Diplômes*, vii. 50.

had been done, the property was divided, usually equally, between the abbey and the tenant.[1]

Besides agricultural land, Cluny came to own a considerable number of churches. These had been constructed by private owners, or usurped by them in the troubled times of the Norman and Hungarian invasions. Such owners held them like any other kind of private property; and when they passed to the abbey by benefaction they continued to be held by a like tenure.[2]

The development of the Cluny estate brought the abbey for the first time into the feudal courts,[3] where it was generally represented by its provost. The abbey lands at Vergisson, given by one Adalard, gave rise to the earliest litigation. In 947 the provost and sacristan of Cluny, accompanied by vassals and serfs of the abbey, appeared before Letald, Count of Mâcon, and his court to maintain their rights on the land against a certain Walter. The title-deeds of both parties were read, and those of Cluny were judged valid as being the older.[4] In the next year there was another action, as two sisters claimed that they rightfully owned half the church at Vergisson; but again the abbey's charters won the day.[5] Such actions are typical of many,[6] and serve to show the advantage that continuity of ownership and the adequate custody of its archives gave the abbey over the private owner of land.

With advancing years Aymar became blind, and chose as his successor Maiol, a scholarly and charming Southerner, educated in the schools of Lyons, who had entered Cluny after holding a canonry at Mâcon. Unlike the puny Odo and the humble Aymar, he was beautiful in person: his disciple Odilo describes him as 'ingressu gravis, voce sublimis, ore facundus, visu jocundus, vultu angelicus, aspectu serenus, in omni motu, gestu, vel actu corporis, honestatem praesentans'.[7] Yet he possessed the monastic virtue of humility,

[1] Valous, p. 382.
[2] For the parallel situation in England see Pollock and Maitland, i, pp. 497 et seqq.
[3] The earlier Benedictine idea had been that a monk, or his community, should not bring an action, and that he should only appear in court exceptionally, as a witness to the truth.
[4] *Chartes et Diplômes*, vii. 135.   [5] Ibid., vii. 158.
[6] See Pignot, i. 230; *Chartes et Diplômes*, vii. 231, 249; *Ann. Bened.*, iii. 507.
[7] Marrier, 284.

and was unwilling to assume the abbatial dignity. But such unwillingness to submit to the will of the brethren was itself a kind of pride, and in the end Maiol was forced [1] to assent to his election; poor blind Aymar himself took him by the hand and led him to the Abbot's throne.

He continued Aymar's work in consolidating the temporal position of Cluny,[2] and carried on the reforming task of Odo. Like him, he did little to increase the number of monasteries dependent on Cluny,[3] but was content to reform and restore Benedictine monasteries without bringing them into formal relation with Cluny. In such wise he reformed Saint-Honorat-de-Lérins, Marmoutiers, Saint-Germain-d'Auxerre,[4] Saint-Maur-des-Fossés,[5] Saint-Pierre-le-Vif at Sens, which had relapsed after its reform by Odo,[6] and Saint-Bénigne-de-Dijon.[7] His reforms extended outside France; he became the confidant of the Emperor Otto I and his wife Adelaide of Burgundy, and stayed much in Italy, both in its Benedictine monasteries and at court. In 966 the Emperor and Empress confided to him the monastery of Sant' Apollinare in Classe at Ravenna[8]; and he also reformed San Pietro al Ciel d'Oro at Pavia, that had relapsed once more since Odo's reforma-

[1] 'Electus advocatur, invitatus restitit, rogatus contradicit, adiuratus tremiscit, interdictus quiescit.' Marrier, 284.
[2] See Sackur, i. 215. In 946 he obtained from Pope Agapitus a confirmation of the abbey's privileges under its foundation charter, extending the privilege of exemption from the dominion of King, Bishop, Lord, or any of William's kinsmen, to any lands that the abbey might acquire (Marrier, 6). He built a new church for the abbey, that under the name of Saint-Pierre-le-Vieux survived until the Revolution; and he rebuilt the priory of Saint-Marcel-lès-Chalon given to Cluny by Geoffrey Grisegonelle, Count of Anjou (Pignot, i. 273).
[3] When he became abbot only five monasteries were subject to Cluny—Souvigny, Romainmôtier, Sauxillange, and Saint-Jean and Saint-Martin at Mâcon. The abbey's possession of Charlieu was still in dispute (Pignot, i. 412; Sackur, i. 215). Besides Saint-Marcel-lès-Chalon (Sackur, ii. 39), the only monasteries added were those of Saint-Marcel-de-Sauzet, given by Lambert, Count of Valence, in 985 (Pignot, i. 273; Sackur, i. 232); Saint-André-de-Rosans, given in 988 (Sackur, ii. 81); Arluc and Montmajour, which had been devastated by the Saracens (Sackur, i. 230); and Saint-Amand, on the left bank of the Rhone, the seat of a small and unimportant priory (Sackur, i. 229). The land at Payerne was given to Cluny in his day, but the monastery was only built under his successor.
[4] Sackur, i. 243. A Cluniac monk of Italian birth was installed as Abbot.
[5] The reform of most of these was undertaken at the Pope's request (Pignot, i. 272 et seq.).
[6] Ibid., i. 280.
[7] Through its abbot, St. Guillaume de Dijon, who had been at Cluny under Maiol, similar reforms were extended to Fécamp, Fruttuaria, Saint-Épire-de-Toul, and other monasteries (ibid., i. 480 et seqq.; Marrier, 298).
[8] Sackur, i. 227, gives the date of its reformation as 971.

tion, and San Salvatore in the same city.¹ After the death of Otto, Maiol was summoned to Rome to advise his son Otto II, but as a consequence of the Emperor's treatment of his mother, Maiol soon broke with him, refusing his offer of the Papal tiara.² On one of his journeys from Italy he was captured by Saracens at the bridge of Orcières on the Drac, and had to be ransomed by Cluny at great cost.³

He died at Souvigny in 994 on his way to reform the royal abbey of Saint-Denis, to which Hugh Capet had summoned him.⁴ His greatest contribution to Cluny was a new insistence on Charity as the foundation virtue of monastic life; and it is perhaps not unworthily that he figures as one of the Cluniac saints.⁵ Hugh Capet came twice as a pilgrim to his tomb at Souvigny, wearing in place of the royal mantle the cloak of Saint Martin, and so long as he stayed in the monastery following the Cluniac Rule as humbly and faithfully as had Maiol himself.⁶

Three years before his death Maiol had appointed a monk of Cluny, Odilo, as his coadjutor,⁷ and he succeeded him as Abbot. A member of the Auvergnat family of Mercœur, he had been admitted when very young to the noble Chapter of Brioude; but, drawn by his friendship with Maiol, had left it in 987 for Cluny.⁸ Like Odo, he was physically a weakling, small, thin, and pale, but full of energy; and like Odo he combined the power of commanding men with monastic humility. From Maiol he inherited a tradition of mercy and charity: 'etiamsi damnandus sim, malo tamen de misericordia quam ex duritia vel crudelitate damnari'.⁹

It was under Odilo that the abbey of Cluny entered upon the greatest period of its temporal history. Already in 990,

¹ Pignot, i. 253; L. M. Smith, 105; Sackur, i. 236.
² Pignot, i. 267; Sackur, i. 233.
³ This story is sometimes dismissed as legend; but it is recorded by Odilo, Maiol's disciple and successor (Marrier, 295).
⁴ Its discipline had become so far relaxed that the abbey had renounced the Benedictine for the easier Augustinian Rule. The reform was completed by Odilo after Maiol's death (Pignot, i. 310; Sackur, ii. 32).
⁵ His tomb at Souvigny was long a place of pilgrimage; he has still an altar there. His robe became a relic used for the cure of sterility.   ⁶ Pignot, i. 311.
⁷ *Vita Odilonis.* Marrier, 317. Maiol was careful to have the election formally made by the Chapter, in the presence of the Archbishop of Lyons, the bishops of Geneva, Lausanne, Mâcon, and Autun; and of five other abbots. It was by far the most formal election that had hitherto been held.
⁸ Ibid., 317.   ⁹ Ibid., 318.

while Maiol yet lived, he had obtained from the Council of Anse confirmation of the abbey's possession of Charlieu, and a general anathema against all those who encroached on the abbey's property: against those who plundered and stole in its churches, houses, and cellars; against lords and soldiers who built castles or encamped upon its territory; against men who carried off its cattle or ravaged its crops.[1] Ten years later he obtained from King Robert and from Henry, Duke of Burgundy, a deed that forbade any man, even prince or duke, to build castles or fortresses within the bounds of the abbey estate.[2] Pope Gregory V not only confirmed the ancient privileges of the abbey, but also asserted its right to choose any bishop to perform the consecration of its churches and the ordination of its priests and Abbots: a privilege directly aimed against the local rights of the Bishop of Mâcon.[3] In 1016 Benedict VIII confirmed all the privileges of the abbey and extended them to all its dependent houses in Burgundy, Aquitaine, and Provence.[4] Like his predecessors Odilo reformed many monasteries; but unlike them he tended to make these monasteries subject to Cluny. It is with him that the idea of a Cluniac *Order* may be said to begin: a substitution for the Benedictine idea of monastic autonomy of the conception of a congregation of monasteries all owing allegiance to a single abbey, their government all ultimately controlled by its Abbot. The conception is a reflection of a time when with the progress of civilization the whole social fabric was being gradually organized on a larger scale: when kingdoms were being built up out of duchies, when great estates were being brought together out of lesser holdings, when the foundations of feudal integration were being laid. The idea of a Cluniac Order was

[1] Pignot, i. 387. None the less in 1016 Benedict VIII had to address a letter to several Bishops of France calling upon many lords who had encroached on the feudal privileges of Cluny to repent and repair the evil by Michaelmas or to come under his ban and the excommunication of their priests (ibid. i. 339).

[2] *Chartes et Diplômes*, xx. 229. The limits fixed are 'A civitate Cabilonensi (Chalon) et Matiscensi (Mâcon) et Monte Algoio (? Montgely) et castro Chedelensi (? Chedde) et Monte Sancti Vincenti (Mont-Saint-Vincent)'.

[3] Letonnelier, 25.

[4] Ibid., 31. These privileges came to be regarded as so typical that in 1079 Gregory VII, addressing the monks of Saint-Victor-de-Marseille, declared that he gave them confirmation of an exemption as wide as that of the abbey of Cluny. The same formula was used a little later for the exemption of the monastery of Hirschau (ibid., 23).

evolved as gradually as these; and for a time its evolution seems to have been scarcely realized.

The Empress Adelaide gave to Odilo the monastery of St. Victor at Geneva,[1] and further endowed her mother's gift of Payerne; in 995 Walter, Bishop of Autun, gave the little monastery of Mesvres,[2] near his cathedral city; in 998 one Rodolf gave Cluny a monastery of St. Peter he built at Bévais, on the lake of Neufchâtel[3]; and the sons of Odilo's four brothers founded and built a monastery for twenty-five monks at La Voulte.[4] Quite close to Cluny another important monastery was established at Paray, given to Odilo by Hugh, Count of Chalon and Bishop of Auxerre, and endowed with the market of Mont-Saint-Vincent and all its rights and dues.[5] In 1010 Saint-André-de-Gap was given to Cluny,[6] in 1026 the great abbey of Vézelay came under Cluniac rule,[7] in 1030 Amadeus I of Savoie-Belley gave Malaucène,[8] in 1038 Ambierle was added; and these were far from being the only acquisitions.[9]

In 1014 the Emperor Henry came to Cluny, and dedicated at the altar not only the sceptre, orb, and crown of his coronation and a great cross of gold, but also estates in Alsace to increase the abbey revenues.

As a consequence of such benefactions Odilo had occasion to become a great building Abbot. He restored Payerne and Nantua, enlarged Romainmôtier, built the monastic buildings of St. Victor at Geneva, built the monasteries of Saint-Flour, Paray, Souvigny, and Ambierle, and repaired Charlieu and Sauxillange.[10] At Cluny itself 'he marvellously adorned the cloisters with columns and marble brought from the farthermost parts of the province,'[11] and he built a splendid gate for the Abbey (Fig. X), modelled on the Roman Porte d'Arroux at Autun.[12] He is said to have modified the

[1] Pignot, i. 323; Sackur, ii. 77.
[2] Pignot, i. 315; Sackur, ii. 37. Some of the monastic buildings are still in existence; the tower, all that remained of the church, fell down in 1836.
[3] Pignot, i. 322; Sackur, ii. 79.   [4] Sackur, ii. 58.
[5] Pignot, i. 317. Under the shelter of the monastery a flourishing town grew up. The beginnings of the monastery go back to 973 (Sackur, i. 241), but it does not appear to have been definitely Cluniac until May 999 (Sackur, ii. 40.)
[6] Sackur, ii. 82.   [7] Ibid., ii. 38.   [8] Ibid., ii. 80.
[9] Others were Nantua, Saint-Flour, Sainte-Colombe near Toulouse (Sackur, ii. 83).
[10] *Vita Jotsaldi*, i, cap. xiii.   [11] Ibid., i, cap. xi.
[12] It originally had an upper story with an arcaded gallery.

FIG. II

MONASTIC HOUSES IN FRANCE, BELGIUM AND SWITZERLAND DIRECTLY DEPENDENT ON THE ABBEY OF CLUNY

Based on a list compiled soon after 1349 printed in Marrier, Bibliotheca Cluniacensis, col. 1705–52. The dependencies of the daughterhouses are omitted. Certain houses that had formerly belonged to the Order but had freed themselves by this date are added

NOT IDENTIFIED

Prioratus de Magobrio, dioc. Autun (? Mauvron, Nièvre).

Prioratus S. Petri de Aqualia, dioc. Liège (? Acq. Pas de Calais).

Prioratus de Ymmonte, dioc. Belley.

Prioratus B. Mariae de Ulmatis, alias de Casanova, dioc. Apt (? Notre Dame de Caseneuve, Gard).

Prioratus S. Helenae (no diocese given) (? Sainte Hélène sur Lot, Lozère).

Prioratus S. Joannis Doureau, dioc. Valence or Die.

Prioratus de Brosiliis, Poitou or Saintonge.

Prioratus de Manomena.

Prioratus de Sardone, dioc. Constance.

Prioratus B. Mariae de Bosco.

Prioratus de Thiescourt, dioc. Bâle.

Prioratus de Ysteim, dioc. Constance.

Prioratus de Orthovillarii, dioc. Lausanne.

OFF MAP

Feldbach, on Lake Constance.

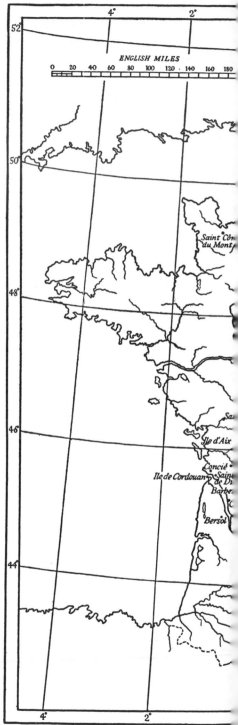

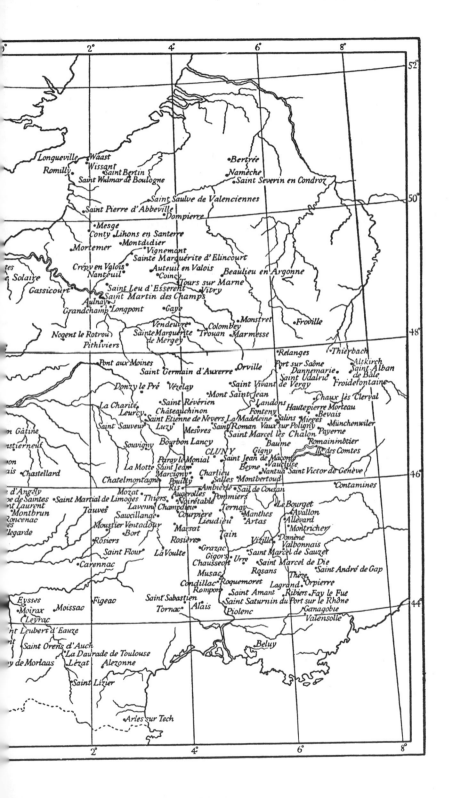

Augustan boast and to have declared: 'I found an abbey of wood, I leave an abbey of marble.'[1]

Already, too, provision had to be made for monks travelling from one monastery to another, or to some district where the abbey's interests called them; and *mansiones* or hostels were established at Vienne, Viviers, Avignon, and Arles, where in default of a priory of Cluny its monks might find shelter.[2]

Towards the end of Odilo's life the extension of the Cluniac Order, and the spread of its reforms outside the Order, led to the codification of the Customs of Cluny— the usages and conventions of monasticism that had grown up within the framework of the Benedictine rule.[3]

The agricultural lands of Cluny were greatly increased under Odilo's rule. In the four years between 1027 and 1030, for example, the abbey received thirty-one donations of land.[4] Such gifts were made on a man's taking monastic vows, on the oblation of infants, and on a man's entering the abbey for death and burial.[5] One charter describes how Guichard, seigneur of Roffey, a hamlet belonging to Cluny, was brought into the abbey past speech and at point of death: his relations decided what must be done for the salvation of his soul, and gave the abbey land at Surgnon and some of which the abbey already disputed the possession at Roffey itself.[6] Gifts of land were also made in reparation for sins committed by the donor, his ancestors, or his descendants; there are three instances of such gifts in reparation for murder, and one for a kick to a serf.[7] Sometimes the abbey owed some return to the donor for his benefaction: in 1013, for instance, one Atto gave the abbey possession of serfs, woods, and land in the villages of Curtil, Buffières, and Mont Serein, on condition that the monks should give him their

---

[1] The Cluniac *Consuetudines* written for Farfa (ed. Albers, 139) describe the monastery buildings as he left them. Some of the early work can still be traced in the seventeenth-century plan of the abbey, published by M. Virey (*Millénaire*, ii. 231).

[2] Pignot, i. 221.

[3] The earliest surviving account of these *consuetudines*, drawn up for the use of the monastery of Farfa, was written between 1039 and 1049. See Chapter V. Farfa had been reformed soon after 998 by the advice of Odilo and William, Abbot of Saint Bénigne-de-Dijon. See V. Mortet, 'Note sur la date de rédaction des *Coutumes de Cluny* dites de Farfa', in *Millénaire*, i. 142.

[4] Valous, p. 342.   [5] Ibid., 328; *Chartes et Diplômes*, xvii. 53 and xxviii. 253.

[6] Ibid., xv. 18.   [7] Valous, p. 327.

protection and provide him for the rest of his life with all necessities of food and clothing.[1] Similarly land was often given subject to a life-interest in favour of the donor and his wife or children or some other third party.[2] Such gifts were of every kind: uncultivated land, isolated fields and meadows, fishing-rights,[3] forests, vineyards, farms with their serfs, villages, freeholds, feudal fiefs, even castles. The abbey had already the practice of letting lands as *precaria*, and under Odilo the practice was developed to include the actual granting of fiefs.[4]

Cluny, indeed, began to play its part in the feudal world as a whole, as it had already done in the private counsels of King and Emperor. Though it formed part of that world, it was yet outside and above its petty quarrels and military ambitions, and thus came naturally to fill the role of mediator and arbitrator in feudal quarrels. Out of such mediation two institutions of real importance arose: the *Pax Dei* and the *Truga Dei*.

The first was instituted at a synod held at the Cluniac daughter house of Sauxillange between 995 and 1005. Archambaud II of Bourbon and Landry II of Nevers were at war over the possession of certain lands between the Loire and the Allier, one supporting the claims of King Robert to Burgundy and the other those of his father-in-law, Otho-Guillaume. The war was embittered and its devastations widespread. To bring it to an end, the Bishops of Le Puy, Viviers, Valence, and Clermont, and a great concourse of barons and lesser folk, swore a solemn agreement.

'Since we know that without peace no man may see God, we adjure you, in the name of the Lord, to be men of peace, that henceforward in these bishoprics and in these counties no man may break into a church, nor bear off the horses, foals, oxen, cows, asses, sheep, goats or pigs of the labourer and the serf, or the burden he bears upon his shoulders; that no man may kill any of these beasts; that he may exact nothing except from his own

---

[1] Valous, p. 331.
[2] Loc. cit. Sometimes a trifling rent was paid—a few measures of corn or a few baskets of grapes.
[3] In 1017 William V of Aquitaine gave Cluny half the *cens* paid him by the fishermen of the Ile de Ré (Pignot, i. 409), and the abbey also held rights of salmon-fishing in the Loire and rights in other rivers (Valous, p. 360).
[4] Ibid., p. 377.

servants and his immediate dependants; that to build or to assault
a fortress he may only take the men of his own land, his allod,
bénéfice or *commende*; that clerks may not bear arms borne by laymen; that no man may ever insult a monk, or those who walk with
him, if they are unarmed; that no man may dare to invade the
lands of churches, cathedrals, chapters, or monasteries, or to
waylay their agents and despoil them. May every thief and evil-
doer who infringes this or refuses to observe it, be excommunicate,
anathema, and driven from the threshold of the church, until he
make amends; and if he refuse, let the priest refuse to sing mass for
him, or to celebrate any sacrament; and at his death let him be
deprived of Christian burial.' [1]

The deed was confirmed by the Archbishops of Bourges and
Vienne, and served to establish a precedent that helped to
restrain the devastations of feudal warfare.

Out of the *Pax Dei* grew the *Truga Dei*, which particu-
larized its provisions and made them generally applicable.
Hugh of Flavigny records how Odilo and his friend Richard,
Abbot of Saint-Venne at Verdun, persuaded both Austria
and Neustria to accept it. [2] In 1042 the Truce of God was
proclaimed in all the dioceses of France; and Odilo and the
bishops of the south addressed a letter to the bishops of
Italy, asking them to adopt the measure and enumerating
its provisions. [3]

'From the hour of vespers on Wednesday until sunrise on
Monday let there reign a settled peace and an enduring truce between all Christians, friends and enemies, neighbours and strangers,
so that for these four days and five nights at all hours there may be
safety for all men, so that they can devote themselves to business
without fear of attack. Let those who, having pledged themselves
to the truce, break it, be excommunicated, accursed, and abomi-
nated, now and forever, unless they repent and make amends.
Whosoever shall kill a man on a day of truce, shall be banished

---

[1] Mabillon, *De re diplomatica*, vi. 577; Guépratte, p. 300; Pignot, i. 394. On Cluny
and the Peace movement see L. M. Smith, p. 181 et seqq. On the Peace movement
in general see Pfister, *Études sur le règne de Robert le Pieux*, p. 165; L. Huberti, *Studien
zur Rechtsgeschichte der Gottesfrieden und Landfrieden*, Ansbach 1892, vol. i, 'Die
Friedensordnungen in Frankreich; A. Krey, 'The International State of the Middle
Ages', in *American Historical Review*, xxviii, 1922, p. 3; and L. C. Mackinney, 'The
People and public opinion in the eleventh century Peace movement', in *Speculum*, v,
1930, p. 181.
[2] *Chronicon Virdunense*, in Labbé, *Bibliotheca nova*, i, p. 187.
[3] Mansi, *Concilia*, xix. 593.

and driven out of his country, and shall make his way into exile at Jerusalem. . . .'[1]

Another institution of Odilo's yet lives. On All Saints' Day the bells of the Charollais still ring from vespers into the night, in commemoration of the dead. For more than nine centuries they have rung, since Odilo in 998 instituted the solemn commemoration of the dead of his order on the day following All Saints' Day.[2] When on All Souls' Day we remember and pray for our dead, we are but making universal the love and remembrance that Odilo had for his dead brethren of Cluny.

Odilo's reign brought prosperity to the abbey, but such prosperity was not unclouded. In the year 1033 Cluny began to suffer from a great famine, of which Radulphus Glaber has left a vivid description.[3] For three years the ground was so water-logged that it could not be ploughed and sown, and the meadow hay could not be got in. At harvest-time weeds covered the fields; the measure of grain cost sixty sous, and rich and poor alike were starving. Men ate beasts and birds, twigs of trees, and water-weed; and there were stories of men eating human flesh[4] and even murdering for food. In the Mâconnais men mixed a white clayey earth with barley-meal to make bread, and went pale and haggard, their skins puffy and swollen, their voices thin and like the cry of a dying bird. Men died by hundreds; five hundred were buried in the same grave; and wolves came after the unburied dead. Men heard that other provinces were in better state, and started thither, to die by the wayside. Even if they got food, it was often too late; they had no strength to assimilate it, and sometimes died in the effort of carrying it to their lips.

All turned to the abbey for help; but if its charity was inexhaustible, its means were limited. It depended alike for

---

[1] The letter goes on to say that these days have been consecrated, Thursday in memory of the Ascension, Friday of the Passion, Saturday of the Burial, and Sunday of the Resurrection.

[2] Marrier, 338. The institution was for Cluny and all its houses, with the clause 'and if anyone else takes our pious institution for example, may he by this very deed become a participant in all the prayers made'.

[3] *Hist.*, Bk. IV, cap. 4. He tells us that the famine started in the East, spread from Greece to Italy and thence to France and England.

[4] It was cooked and put up for sale in Tournus market, but the man who sold it was hanged and burned.

the sustenance of its monks and the provision of its alms upon the crops and produce of its lands; and like its dependents, its monks were starving. All its granaries were emptied; all its treasures and the ornaments of its church were sold to the Jews; even the imperial orb dedicated by Henry II was sacrificed for the poor.[1] When all was spent, the monks begged as best they could, until at last, after three hopeless years, kindly seasons brought back good harvests; and Cluny, like the rest of the world, could return to normal ways.

Like Maiol, Odilo died on a journey; he was at Souvigny when a sudden malady laid him low. As he lay on his bed of sickness he made the friend who watched over him calculate upon an abacus how often he had celebrated mass; he could not recall a single day since his ordination, in spite of illness and of his endless journeys to his monasteries, to Councils, to Rome and to the Emperor's Court, on which he had failed to celebrate the Eucharist. On Christmas Eve he gave in Chapter a most moving sermon on the mystery of the Nativity, and for the last time absolved and blessed the brethren, bidding them honour the feast day with spiritual joy, with no anxious thought for him. On Christmas morning he had his pallet moved into the Chapel of the Virgin and strove to follow all the offices. For some days he lingered, until on the Eve of the Circumcision he died, as befitted a monk, on a bed of ashes. For fifty years he had ruled Cluny wisely and well. Like Maiol he was buried at Souvigny in the presence of the monks of Cluny, Sauxillange, Paray, La Voulte, Thiers, and of all the other brethren who could reach his grave in time; and in after years many were healed at his tomb.[2]

Odilo had refused to nominate his successor, saying that he trusted to the will of God and the election of the brethren. Their choice fell upon Hugh of Semur, a member of a great family of the Brionnais. As a boy he had been sent to continue his studies at the Cluniac house of Saint-Marcel-lès-Chalon, and there, at the age of fifteen, he had entered the noviciate against his father's wish. He was transferred thence to Cluny, where he became Grand Prior while still young. Odilo had died while he was at the court of the

<hr />

[1] Pignot, i. 385.   [2] Marrier, 327; Pignot, i. 443.

Emperor Henry III, acting as the abbey's agent in negotia-
tions in favour of Payerne; and on his return he was unani-
mously elected Abbot.[1]

He was pre-eminently a statesman; and for full sixty
years he governed the Cluniac Order as a wise statesman
governs a kingdom. He did more than this: at every turn of
contemporary history his figure is to be seen standing as
counsellor beside King, Emperor, or Pope—at the French
Court, at Rome, in the Imperial palace at Cologne, in Hun-
gary on the Pope's business, watching the humiliation of
the Emperor at Canossa. And such work, if it lay outside
the formal duties of an abbot, did much to increase the
greatness of the monastery alike in spiritual influence and in
temporal wealth. Most of all it increased the prestige and
power of the Abbot himself. The early Abbots had had to
lead the common life—to follow the daily devotions, to
sleep in the common dormitory, to give the signal for rising,
to eat in the common refectory, to keep silence in certain
places and at certain hours.[2] But the increasing part that the
Abbots came to play in public life gradually loosened and
finally released the bonds of these obligations, and, by the
time of Hugh, the Abbot of Cluny, in virtue of his greatness,
was to some extent above the discipline of its *consuetudines*.
At the same time his power over the other monasteries of
the order was defined and increased. His legislative, judicial
and administrative powers were extended over them as over
Cluny itself.[3] Such power, moreover, was sanctioned and
confirmed by the Pope: '. . . ut priores, monachi ejusdem
ordinis ubilibet commorantes ac loca eorum . . . subjecta sint
abbati Cluniacensi in spiritualibus et temporalibus pleno jure,
promittantque ipsi abbati, quoties novus institutur, obedien-
tiam, manualem et benedictionem recipiant ab eodem et
reddant ad mandatum ipsius abbatis de singulis quae ad
administrationem spiritualem et temporalem pertinent.'[4]
The superior of every Cluniac house, however powerful,

[1] *Vita S. Hugonis*, by Hildebert of Le Mans: Marrier, 416. The election was unani-
mous and formal. Lives of him were written by the Cluniac monks Gilon and
Etzelon (on which another life by Hildebert of Le Mans was based) and by his
nephew Raynald, who was Abbot of Vézelay.
[2] Dom Besse, 'L'ordre de Cluny et son gouvernement', in *Revue Mabillon*, i, 1905,
p. 6.
[3] Ibid., p. 8.   [4] Ibid., p. 9.

was nominated by the Abbot of Cluny; the profession of every member of the Order, even in distant lands, was made in his name and with his sanction. All abbeys restored or reformed by Cluny had to enter the Order and become its dependents, though certain great abbeys that voluntarily adopted Cluniac customs were free to remain outside the Order.[1] The dependent abbeys, however ancient, were definitely reduced to a subordinate rank[2]; the catalogue of the Abbots of Sauxillange records 'Decimus Hugo de Mercorio, abbas et prior, 1060, quia tunc reducta est abbatia in prioratum, per S. Hugonem Magnum'.[3] The practice was confirmed and sanctioned by Pope Gregory VII in 1076[4] and by Pope Paschal II in 1100: all subject abbeys were to be reduced to the rank of priories, except for eleven which, because of their ancient glory, were to be permitted to keep the title of abbey.[5]

A new principle of monasticism was evolved, and in place of an autonomous monastery under its Abbot, an independent Order[6] under a monarchical head was created. The advantages of such a system were quickly appreciated even outside the Order. At the Council of Meaux, held in 1082, the Papal legates, the archbishops of Lyons and Bourges, the Bishops of Châlons-sur-Marne, Amiens, Soissons, Nevers, Langres, Autun, Mâcon, and Grenoble—all of whom had Cluniac priories in their dioceses—concurred in asking that all the lesser abbeys, not sufficiently

---

[1] e.g. Hirschau, La Cava, Sahagun, and Reading. Their affiliation was undefined and its closeness varied. Through the influence of William, Abbot of Hirschau 1068–91, customs derived from Cluny were widely adopted in Germany. (See Heimbucher, *Die Orden und Congregationen*, i. 253–6; and *Festschrift zum Elfhundertjährigen Jubiläum des Deutschen Campo Santo in Rom*, p. 115.) Hermann, Abbot of Saint-Martin de-Tournai 1117–32, wrote that it was hardly possible to find a monastery in France or in Flanders in which the Customs of Cluny were not observed. Luc d'Achery *Spicilegium*, 1723 ed., ii. 913.

[2] e.g. Nantua, Romainmôtier, Ambierle, Charlieu, and Sauxillange.

[3] Quoted Cucherat, p. 24.

[4] *Bullarium Cluniacense*, 18, c. 2.

[5] Gregory excepted Vézelay, Saint-Gilles, Saint-Jean-d'Angély, Saint-Pierre-de-Moissac, Saint-Pierre-de-Maillezais, Saint-Martial-de-Limoges, Saint-Cyprien-de-Poitiers, Monstierneuf, and Saint-Sauveur-de-Figeac. Paschal II added Saint-Germain-d'Auxerre, Saint-Austremoine-de-Mozat, and Saint-Bertin-de-Terouanne (*Bull. Sacr. Ord. Clun.*, p. 32). At Saint-Gilles, Vézelay, and Saint-Bertin the monks elected their Abbot with the consent of the Abbot of Cluny; at Menat, Monstierneuf, Saint-Germain-d'Auxerre and Saint-Martial-de-Limoges the Abbot of Cluny nominated him. Letonnelier, p. 54.

[6] On this title see Migne, *Part. Lat.*, cxlv. 866.

endowed to support twelve monks and an abbot, should be turned into priories subject to Cluny or to Marmoutiers.[1]

Under Hugh, the Cluniac Order was enriched both by new foundations and by the inclusion of ancient monasteries. In 1052[2] Bernard de Chaillent gave Hugh lands on the Loire between Cosne and Nevers on an important route of pilgrimage and trade, and provided for the erection of monastic buildings. A colony of Cluniac monks was established there, who by their splendid generosity and hospitality earned for their monastery the title of La Charité-sur-Loire.[3] Another great new foundation was the monastery of Monstierneuf at Poitiers, founded by William VIII of Aquitaine, who had married a niece of Hugh of Semur.[4] Established in William's own city, it had all the advantages of his protection and interest; its chronicler describes how he never failed to visit it before entering his palace when he returned from a journey, and how he would penetrate into the kitchen to find out from the cellarer if the monks had enough to eat.[5] In return the monks laid his cover and set out his pittance and his measure of wine every day in the refectory, as if the Duke had indeed been their brother. William I of Nevers gave the abbey of Cluny the monastery of St. Stephen he had built in Nevers. In the title-deed he enumerates his benefactions: 'I have built a noble monastery with three towers, very fairly built, as all may see. I have erected the cloister and the monastic buildings, large enough

---

[1] Yepez, iv, p. 331. Too much opposition was encountered to make the plan effective.

[2] According to another account 1056.

[3] 'Pauperes se invicem invitantes: "Eamus," dicebant, "ad sanctorum Karitatem." Unde factum est ut, ex illa et frequenti et diurna invitatione, nomen hujusmodi aptarent loco' (Richardus Cluniacensis, *Chronicon*, in *Gallia Christiania*, xii. 403). It was so called as early as 1052. It was originally called Saint-Cyr. Its superior once borrowed four thousand sous of gold to continue the customary almsgiving at a time of financial difficulty (Pignot, ii. 253). In 1081 Philip Augustus gave the abbey and the citizens living in its shelter the right to wall and fortify the new town, that had already suffered considerably from the neighbouring lord of La Marche (ibid., ii. 248). La Charité came to have a considerable extension abroad: five daughter houses in England, one in Portugal, Civitot in Constantinople, and Santa Croce in Venice (ibid., ii. 254).

[4] To the Dukes of Aquitaine, Cluny owed not only its own foundation but also the foundation of Monstierneuf and the restoration of Maillezais and Saint-Eutrope-de-Saintes.

[5] Martini monachi, *Hist. monast. novi*, in Martène, *Thesaur. Anecdot.*, iii. 1214. If they had only eggs and small fish he would order his treasurer to provide the cost of more nourishing food.

to suffice for the monks who are coming to inhabit them, with a chapel for the sick.' He gave them crosses, gospel-books, chalice and ornaments for the altar, and vestments for the celebrant. The monks owned the *bourg* of Saint-Étienne with all its rights. Any of the count's men that came to live there were to be subject to the Prior, except for services they owed the count; any strangers were to be dependent only on the monastery. The monastery was to have its own shops, its own community of merchants, the right of buying and selling at the Prior's pleasure upon its land, the right of sanctuary, the right of wood-cutting, and the right of exemption for its tenants from military service.[1]

Nearly all the other monasteries included in the Order under Hugh were ancient foundations: Saint-Pierre-de-Moissac, given to Hugh to reform in 1047[2]; Saint-Martial-de-Limoges, given to Cluny (against the will of its monks) after a disastrous fire in 1062[3]; Saint-Eutrope-de-Saintes, Saint-Saulge-de-Valenciennes,[4] Saint-Sauveur-de-Figeac, Saint-Orens-d'Auch, Saint-Pierre-de-Beaulieu,[5] Saint-Alban-de-Bâle, Saint-Wulmar-d'Unicourt.

Between 1050 and 1060 councils were held at Toulouse and in Provence to protest against the usurpation of Church property by laymen. In consequence, many owners renounced their rights over churches and monasteries, which were reformed, often under the protection of some great abbey.[6] Isarn de Lavaur, Bishop of Toulouse, confided to Cluny the reformation of the chief churches of his city[7]: Sainte-Marie-de-la-Daurade, that after some resistance became a Cluniac priory; Saint-Étienne, where the Augustinian rule was re-established[8]; Saint-Sernin, that was made a Cluniac priory but with Papal support recovered its independence as an Augustinian house.[9]

Centule II, Count of Béarn, in 1077 gave Sainte-Foy-de-

[1] Pignot, ii. 256. Much the same privileges were granted by William of Aquitaine to Monstierneuf.
[2] Ibid., ii. 189.
[3] Ibid., ii. 211. For its earlier connexion with Cluny see p. 10.
[4] Marrier, 535.   [5] Ibid., 525.
[6] Pignot, ii. 189. Besides churches the abbey was given a certain number of canonical prebends (Pignot, i. 222).   [7] Ibid., ii. 199.
[8] It later became a priory dependent on Moissac.
[9] Pignot, ii. 200.

Morlaas to Cluny and Moissac, in expiation of a marriage within the prohibited degrees.[1] Two years later Philip Augustus gave Cluny the church of Saint-Martin-des-Champs at Paris, that had been magnificently restored by his father.[2] Mozat, one of the most ancient abbeys in France, was affiliated to Cluny in 1095 [3]; and in 1100 the ancient abbey of Saint-Germain-d'Auxerre, that had relapsed since its reformation by Maiol, was set under Cluny by Urban II. In the same year Hugh was given charge of the abbey of Saint-Bertin near Térouanne, that dated from the middle of the seventh century.[4] In 1103 the monastery of Vézelay, founded by the epic hero Gérard of Roussillon, was attached to Cluny by Pascal II.[5]

A new foundation of another kind was the first nunnery of the Order, founded at Marcigny at the instance of Hugh by his brother Geoffrey II of Semur; their sister Ermengarde was appointed as its first Prioress.[6] It was established for ninety-nine nuns—a number never exceeded—with Our Lady, 'Notre Dame Abbesse', as the invisible hundredth. A seat was kept for her in church, a portion was set for her at every meal and afterwards given to the poor. Some of the nuns were cloistered, living in common; some were enclosed in cells.

'The world being dead to them, they were dead to the world, and becoming unseen by all, after their vocation they laid over their eyes and faces a thick veil, like a shroud; they wore it until their death, as a symbol that should for ever remind them of their latter end and warn them to prepare for it. Enclosed in this cloister of salvation, or rather buried alive in this sepulchre, they waited to change a temporary prison for the freedom of eternity, and to change their burial for resurrection.'

The vow of seclusion was most strictly kept. Once the nunnery buildings caught fire, and the flames were licking the roofs of the nuns' cells. The inhabitants of the village roused the Archbishop of Lyons, a Papal Legate, who was

[1] Pignot, ii. 197.
[2] Marrier, 527; Pignot, ii. 271. By the thirteenth century it had twenty-six priories in France and three in England.
[3] Marrier, 533.
[4] Ibid., 538. The abbey finally succeeded in freeing itself from Cluny in 1138.
[5] Pignot, ii. 262.
[6] *Chartes et Diplômes*, xxxii, p. 190. It was founded in 1056 and was in being by 1061.

staying near by: he entered the cloister and besought them to flee from peril, by his authority and by their obedience. A noble sister named Gisla made answer: 'My father, the fear of God and the command of our Abbot keep us enclosed within these limits until we die. Under no pretext, in no circumstances, can we pass the bounds assigned to our penitence, unless he who enclosed us in the name of the Lord should himself permit it. Therefore order us not to do that which is forbidden; but rather command the fire to draw back in the name of our Lord Jesus Christ.' And at the Legate's prayer the flames were stayed.[1]

To secure the complete enclosure of the nuns there was attached to the nunnery a priory of monks,[2] who acted as the priests and spiritual directors of the nuns and looked after the temporal affairs of the nunnery. Many noble ladies, including Adela of Blois, the daughter of William the Conqueror, there took the veil[3]; and a bull of Urban II enumerates seven dependent nunneries in France, one in England, and one in Spain.

Under Abbot Hugh the Order of Cluny was established in both Italy, England, and Spain. The Order had taken some part in the organization of the Burgundian crusades against the Saracens of Spain,[4] and the relation was made closer by the ties of blood that existed between Hugh and the Spanish rulers.[5] Alonzo VI of Castille received Hugh as one of his most honoured counsellors,[6] and became one of

---

[1] Pet. Ven., de Mirac., i. 22; Marrier, 1280.

[2] First 12 in number, then 30. Pignot, ii. 34. Marcigny, however, can hardly be called a 'double' monastery in the usual sense. The buildings were separate; the church only was common, with a wooden screen to separate the monks from the nuns.

[3] For a list see Dijon MS. fonds Baudot 1018, p. 117. Some are enumerated in Cucherat, 68–71.

[4] In 1033 Odilo had enrolled men for the Crusade, who gave part of their booty to Cluny. Rad. Glab., Hist., Bk. IV, cap. 7. On the whole question see Petit, Croisades bourguignonnes. M. Bédier gives the Liber S. Jacobi a Cluniac origin (Legéndes Épiques, iii, pp. 89 et seqq.), but his arguments are hardly conclusive. It is true that the four routes he mentions all include Cluniac houses among their stopping-places—the first Saint-Gilles, the second Moissac, the third Vézelay, the fourth Saint-Jean-d'Angély and Saint-Eutrope-de-Saintes (Mâle, Art religieux du XIIᵉ siècle en France, p. 291); but in some places where there were important Cluniac houses these are not mentioned. At Toulouse the (then Augustinian) Saint-Sernin and not La Daurade is commended to the attention of the traveller; at Limoges Saint-Léonard and not Saint-Martial is mentioned; and at Poitiers Saint-Hilaire and not Monstierneuf.

[5] His niece was Queen of Castille, and he had many kinsmen among the Crusaders.

[6] He had owed the taking of Toledo to the intervention of Hugh's cousin, Eudes

Cluny's greatest benefactors. He gave Cluny the monaste of S. Isidoro de Duegna, S. Jaime de Campomodo, S. Colomba de Burgos, and the cell of the hermits at the foot of Montserrat [1]; Garcia of Navarre founded the monastery of S. Maria in his capital of Najera,[2] and Teresa, widow of Count Gomez Didace, gave Cluny the monastery of S. Zoyle de Carrion.[3]

In Lombardy ten priories and nunneries and seventeen small dependencies were founded or included in the Order between 1068 and 1089.[4] A Cluniac house was even founded in the Holy Land.[5]

With the great increase of the Order[6] during his reign Hugh was of necessity a great builder. In France alone Moissac, Layrac, Saint-Gilles, Uzerche, Beaulieu, Monstierneuf and Saint-Cyprien-de-Poitiers, Saint-Martial-de-Limoges, Saint-Eutrope-de-Saintes, Paray, Marcigny, Vézelay, Saint-Étienne-de-Nevers, La Charité, and Saint-Martin-des-Champs

de Bourgogne, and his own marriage with Constance of Chalon to Hugh himself. Hugh went twice to Spain; his chief task was the substitution of the Roman for the Mozarabic rite.

[1] Pignot, ii. 114.   [2] Ibid., ii. 110.

[3] Ibid.; ii. 115. One MS. volume (Bibliothèque Nationale Coll. Moreau, supp. 283) contains nothing but the charters of Cluniac monasteries in Spain. Other monasteries —Sahagun, S. Salvator d'Ogna, S. Salvator de Leyva and S. Maria de Yrache— followed the Cluniac customs but remained outside the Order.

[4] SS. Marco, Fabiano, and Sebastiano, in a suburb of Lodi, 1068; SS. Gabriele e Raffaelle, in a suburb of Cremona, 1077; S. Paolo d'Argano, 1079; S. Valeriano di Rodobbio, near Vercelli, 1082; S. Jacopo di Puntido, near Brescia, 1087; S. Maiolo, Pavia; Padilorone, near Mantua, 1080; S. Martino delle Colle, 1089. The nunneries were Canturio and S. Colombano. The monastery of La Cava adopted the Cluniac customs, but was not included in the Order (Pignot, ii. 290 et seqq.). The Order might have been earlier extended to England if Hugh had conceded William the Conqueror's request for six of his monks for a payment of a hundred silver pounds a year apiece. Hugh, however, refused it as undignified and unchristian (Marrier, 453). In England the priory of St. Pancras at Lewes was founded in 1177, and was followed by the priories of St. Milburga of Wenlock, and St. Andrew of Northampton, dependencies of La Charité. The later Cluniac houses in England were for the most part dependencies of Saint-Martin-des-Champs and La Charité. See Dom L. Guilloreau, 'Les prieurés anglais de l'Ordre de Cluny', in Millénaire, i. 291. They numbered thirty-five in England and four in Scotland.

[5] About 1100 Tancred Prince of Galilee founded and endowed a monastery of St. Saviour and a Latin hospice on Mount Tabor and gave them to Cluny. The Saracens destroyed them in 1113, but they were rebuilt, only to be completely destroyed by Saladin about 1187 (Pignot, ii. 160).

[6] The houses of the Cluniac Order (and it must be remembered that many of the dependent houses had dependencies of their own) seem never to have attained the number of 2,000 often given. I have counted 937: 836 in France and Switzerland, 26 in Spain, 36 in Italy, and 39 in Great Britain. A distinction must be clearly drawn between the houses and churches belonging to the Order and those 'coniunctae' to Cluny, that is exchanging prayers and obituary rolls. A list of these is given in Bullarium Cluniacense, 215, and has led some readers a tray.

were all a-building in his time; and at Cluny itself the erection of a great new basilica was undertaken at the end of 1088, when Hugh was sixty-five and had ruled over his Order for forty years.[1] The basilica took twenty years to build.[2] The houses and priories of the Order paid their share; many kings and great lords and bishops contributed; the poor people of the district, who owed much to the abbey, brought their offerings. But the chief benefactors were Alfonso VI of Castile, who gave an annual tribute of 2,000 pieces of gold and other magnificent offerings,[3] and Henry I of England, who in 1131 gave an annual *cens* of sixty marks on the revenues of London, and forty marks on those of Lincoln.[4] Henry's daughter, the Empress Matilda, gave the new basilica its bells, cast in England of a different metal from that used for the bells of France.[5]

Hugh planned and built a church with a great central nave of eleven bays, double aisles, and two transepts[6]; with a rounded apse surrounded by an ambulatory with five apsidal chapels radiating from it. The nave was two hundred and

[1] The Consuetudines written for Farfa (ed. Albers, p. 139) describe the earlier church as being 140 feet long, 40 feet high, with 160 glazed windows. It was preceded by a narthex or Galilee 65 feet long, with no projecting towers in front. Laymen stood here so as not to interfere with the processions of the monks. The legend of the beginning of the new abbey was that a paralysed Abbot of Baume named Gunzo, who had been brought to end his days at Cluny, saw St. Peter, St. Paul, and St. Stephen in a dream. Peter bade him go at once to the Abbot and bid him build a larger church, taking no heed to the cost; and in token of the message he promised to cure Gunzo, to whom he showed by cords the size and plan that the church should have. St. Hugh believed him, and the great work was begun (Marrier, 457). The story is also told in verse (ibid.; 459).

[2] Ibid., 458.

[3] Alfonso's munificence was duly commemorated. During his lifetime the Psalm *Exaudiat* was sung for him every day at tierce, and a prayer said at High Mass. On Holy Thursday thirty poor men had their feet washed and were fed; and at Easter food was given to a hundred more. Each day the King's dinner was served at the High Table in the refectory and afterwards given to the poor. One of the chief altars in the new basilica was regarded as his gift, and he was remembered in every Mass there celebrated, while after his death Mass was said there daily for the peace of his soul. On his anniversary the bells were rung for Vespers and Mass, twelve poor men were fed for a week, and the monks had an extra cup of wine (Pignot, ii. 492).

[4] Ibid., i. 278.   [5] Duckett, *Charters and Records*, ii. 78.

[6] An unusual feature perhaps copied from the basilica of S. Paolo fuori le Mure at Rome. Descriptions of the abbey will be found in the manuscript of Bouché (Bibliothèque Nationale, nouv. acq. français 4336, p. 97), in that published by L'Huillier (*Vie de Saint Hugues*, p. 629), and in Mabillon's *Itinerarium Burgundicum* (*Ouvrages posthumes*, ii. 19). For reproductions of engravings and drawings of it see F. Bruel, *Cluni 910–1910*; and Conant, *Five old prints of the Abbey of Cluny*, where the reader is warned against the inaccuracy of Sagot's engravings. For reconstructions see Conant in *Speculum*, 1929, pp. 168 et seqq.

FIG. III. CLUNY: THE INTERIOR OF THE ABBEY CHURCH

From an engraving by Auvrai after a drawing by Lallemand. *Voyage Pittoresque de la France*, 1787

sixty feet long [1]; from the door to the apse was just over four hundred and fifteen feet. The arches of the nave were pointed; above them ran a double arcade. The barrel vault rested on piers with a fluted pilaster on the side of the nave, and engaged columns on the three other sides. The capitals were richly sculptured with foliage in the Corinthian style. The nave was ninety-two feet high, the first aisle fifty-five feet high, the second thirty; the width of the whole nave was about one hundred and eighteen feet. The first or great transept was surmounted by three towers : one called the 'Clocher de l'Eau Bénite' [2] towards the south, the 'Clocher des Bisans'—where the great bells hung—to the north, and the 'Clocher du Chœur' in the centre. At the crossing of the second or eastern transept was the 'Clocher des Lampes'. The High Altar was beneath the apse, with the Sacred Elements reserved above it hung in a vessel shaped as a golden dove. The monks' choir extended a third of the way down the nave; it was closed by a double screen. On this was set a great crucifix, with a crowned figure of Christ in silver gilt, before which the procession of the monks stopped as they entered the choir. The whole was lit by three hundred and one windows.[3] Its glories are departed; it is only in imagination that we can now realize its splendour of proportion, the deep glow of colour on wall and capital, the shafts of sunshine falling upon the inlaid floor, the altar lights twinkling in the distant apse, the atmosphere heavy with incense and vibrant with music and prayer. One transept remains; and its overpowering height serves to give the scale of the lost whole, while a few capitals survive to show the beauty of its decoration. Otherwise nothing but an indifferent engraving [4] (Fig. III) remains to perpetuate the image of one of the most splendid churches in Christendom. When Mabillon saw it, still complete after nearly six hundred years, he wrote 'Quam si centies videris toties ejus majestatem obstupesces'.

[1] According to Professor Conant's measurements.
[2] In part still standing.
[3] When a narthex was added in 1220 it became the largest church in Christendom, 525 feet—and has since been challenged only by the new St. Peter's, which measures 675.
[4] The priory Church of Paray-le-Monial (Fig. VIII) is a greatly reduced version of it that serves to give some idea of its effect.

The great increase of the Order of Cluny alike in France and beyond France made it a factor of real importance in the medieval world. The life of choir and cloister went on unchanged; but the power of the congregation and of the Abbot at its head became something far greater than Berno or Odo had ever imagined. Such power was only possible with papal support; but at the time when such support was most needed it was forthcoming. It is doubtful whether Gregory VII was ever a monk of Cluny as Radulphus Glaber declares[1]; and certainly a note of criticism sounds in many of his letters to Hugh.[2] Yet at the Council of Rome in 1077 he declared:

'Among all the abbeys beyond the Alps there shines first and foremost that of Cluny, that is under the protection of the Holy See. Under its sainted Abbots it has reached so high a stage of honour and religion that, because of the zeal wherewith God is there served, without doubt it surpasses all other monasteries, even the most ancient.'[3]

When Odon de Lagery, Bishop of Ostia, ascended the papal throne as Urban II, friendship between Rome and Cluny was assured, for he had passed his youth as a monk of Cluny and had first experienced responsibility as its Grand Prior. In 1088, like his predecessors, he confirmed the privileges of Cluny, but with a new and filial love.

'Most holy, most venerable, most beloved father', he wrote to Hugh, 'the prerogative of our love is due to you in especial, by reason of your long loyalty to the Holy See and of the respect that your own piety and that of your community inspires. Neither am I forgetful that I personally am your debtor for the first lessons of monastic life; for it was in your monastery that by the grace of the Holy Spirit I attained a second spiritual birth.'

Henceforward Cluny was freed from the authority of any papal legate, unless sent to the abbey directly and expressly by the Pope; and in the event of any quarrel with the bishops, it was directed that the Abbot should judge the issue with the right of appeal to the Pope, or to his legate appointed for the purpose.[4] In 1095 Urban II travelled to

---

[1] *Hist.*, Lib. V, cap. 1. See L. M. Smith, 'Cluny and Gregory VII', in *English Historical Review*, xxvi, 1911, p. 30.   [2] L. M. Smith, op. cit., p. 29.
[3] *Bull. Clun.*, p. 21.   [4] Pignot, ii. 149.

FIG. IV. THE ABBEY CHURCH OF CLUNY

Drawing made by the Jesuit Father Étienne Martellange in 1617, showing
the Abbey Church and the Narthex, seen from the garden

France to inaugurate the crusade, and his itinerary shows how closely he was preoccupied with Cluniac interests.[1] After visiting the Cluniac priory of Saint-Gilles he reached Cluny[2] on 18 October. For the first time the sovereign Pontiff was the guest of the abbey; and that Pontiff one who had first entered its gates as a novice and had passed the years of his youth within its walls. Fitly enough he consecrated the High Altar and the altar in the apse where the morning Mass was said in the great unfinished basilica; and in his sermon once more affirmed the independence of the abbey and defined and enlarged the abbey boundaries,[3] within which to make an invasion, to fire houses or crops, to steal or to plunder, to make a man prisoner, to strike a blow in anger, to wound or to murder, made the culprit liable to excommunication. He authorized Abbot Hugh to wear pontifical vestments at the Masses and processions of the principal feasts: the jewelled mitre, the wide-sleeved silken dalmatic, gloves of purple silk, and silken shoes embroidered with gold.[4]

From Cluny, Urban II went to its daughter house of Souvigny, which had suffered considerably from the hostility of Archambaud IV de Bourbon and his son Archambaud V, who had tried to usurp the monastery's rights of justice. Archambaud IV had been excommunicated, but though he had repented on his death-bed there had not been time to lift the ban. At his son's request Urban II went to his grave at Montet, and solemnly readmitted the dead man into the

---

[1] For the itinerary see Montalembert, vi, p. 117 note 2.

[2] He travelled by Le Puy, La Chaise-Dieu, Saint-Gilles, Tarascon, Avignon, and Mâcon.

[3] Pignot, ii. 152–3. The limits were: on the side of Berzé, from above the brook Salare at the meeting of the roads to Mazille and Cluny; on the road to Beaujeu, at the cross-roads above the Cellarer's mill beyond Vianges; on the Mazille side, at the meeting of the roads to Mazille and Sainte-Marie-du-Bois; above Roffey, from the top of the Défend to the crossing of the Bésornay and Charolles roads; on the side of Ciergues, at the cross-roads of Turgé; on the Chalon road, at the great chestnut trees above Mary; towards Brancion, at the road to Bennand wood; towards Tournus, at the Longueau brook between Blanot and Donzy; towards Péronne and Laizé, at the three beech trees that mark the boundary between the Cluny wood and that of the Count of Mâcon; towards Igé, at the beeches on the hill of Montmain (Pignot, ii. 153).

[4] Marrier, p. 22. The Bishops objected to the privilege, and Bernard later declared that it was against monastic humility (Pignot, ii. 151). Marbode, Bishop of Rennes, wrote his *De abbate usurpante pontificalia* against the privilege. The privilege was continued in favour of Abbot Pons in 1109, and made a permanent privilege for the Abbots of Cluny for the Great Feasts in 1114. In 1118 it was extended to all solemn or public Masses (Letonnelier, p. 49).

community of the faithful; and then made his son swear to respect the privileges of Souvigny.[1] From Souvigny the Pope went to the Council of Clermont, and thence to the Cluniac monastery of Sauxillange, where he dedicated the abbey church. A few days later he was at Saint-Flour, where he executed deeds in favour of Sauxillange and Marcigny; and from there he proceeded to Uzerche, where he was to have dedicated the church of the Cluniac priory, but was prevented by Bishop Humbald. He spent Christmas at Limoges, and on the last day of the year dedicated the new church of the Cluniac abbey of Saint-Martial. A fortnight later he was at Poitiers, where he dedicated the abbey church of Monstierneuf. Before he left France he visited the Cluniac monasteries of Saint-Jean-d'Angély, Saint-Eutrope-de-Saintes, Layrac, Beaulieu, Moissac, Toulouse, and Saint-Gilles; and had made it evident to the world that the Sovereign Pontiff still regarded himself as a member of the Order of Cluny. A year after his return to Italy he gave the abbey a new privilege, which extended the immunities enjoyed by the mother house to all the houses of the Order.[2]

His successor, Pascal II, had like him passed his youth as a novice at Cluny. From there, Abbot Hugh had sent him to Rome, where he had joined the household of Gregory VII. In 1106 he came to France as Pope, and made a stay of some two months at Cluny. Christmas was always celebrated there with pomp and splendour; but never more splendidly than in 1106, when a Pope, and a Cluniac Pope, spent it in the abbey and took part in its celebration. The privileges and immunities of the abbey were once more confirmed; and when the Pope finally left it he turned to see its roofs and towers for the last time, and blessed it and all who had enriched it with their gifts.[3]

In 1109 Hugh died, full of years and honours.[4]

'Hic venerabile Cluniacensium
Plus priscis patribus ditat Coenobium.

---

[1] Archambaud V did not keep his promise and had to be cited before Urban II shortly afterwards; but after a second renunciation of his claims to the Abbot of Cluny he seems to have kept his word.
[2] Pignot, ii. 164.
[3] Ibid., ii. 180. In March he dedicated the abbey church of La Charité and in May visited Souvigny.   [4] For an account of his death see Marrier, 436.

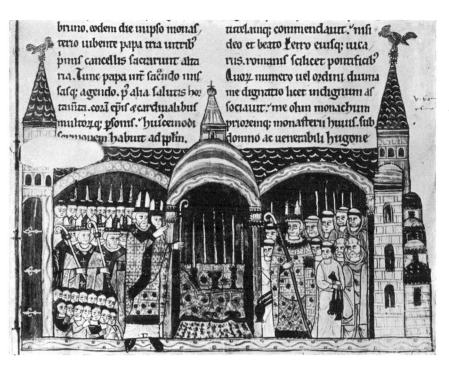

FIG. V. THE CONSECRATION OF THE HIGH ALTAR IN THE ABBEY
CHURCH BY POPE URBAN II IN NOVEMBER 1095

The members of the Papal Court stand behind the Pope, Abbot Hugh and
the monks of Cluny opposite

Illius studio crevit religio,
Crevit et numerus fratrum collegio.
Hanc domum Dominus rebus amplificat
Sic quantum diligat Hugonem indicat,
Beata servitus tot parans redditus
Dum servit, imperat vir Deo subditus.
Non tantum studio contentus, practico
Intendit ocio vitae theoricae:
Marthae sollicitus implet officium,
Audit cum Maria Christi colloquium . . .' [1]

He had ruled the Order with power and wisdom for so long that it was hard to find a successor; and for the first time Cluny had to endure the government of an unworthy Abbot. While Hugh lay dying, the Chapter had elected Pons de Melgueil as his successor, and Hugh confirmed the election.[2] Pons was a splendour-loving noble of the south, who had entered Cluny on the advice of his godfather Pascal II and had become prior of Saint-Martial at Limoges.[3] With his election, division crept into the monastery. He was neither prudent nor spiritual in his administration; he had none of the monastic virtues. In his personal splendour and in his dealings with the world he remained true to the type of feudal baron; he could never, like Odilo and Hugh, become identified with the Order of which he was head.[4] At first circumstances conspired to add to his glory. He made the abbey yet more splendid, rebuilding the cloister and adorning it with sculptured capitals.[5] He acquired its three most precious relics—a fragment of the Cross in 1112, a finger of St. Stephen in 1120, and a tooth of St. John the Baptist, that was hung in a jewelled reliquary to the left of the High Altar. In 1119 Pope Gelasius II, who had fled to France from a Rome too turbulent to be habitable, came to Cluny and died there on a monastic bed of ashes in the middle of the Choir of the abbey church. He was buried with great pomp in the

---

[1] Pet. Ven., *Rythmus de . . . sancto Hugone*. . . . Marrier, 466.
[2] Ordericus Vitalis, *Historia Ecclesiastica*, iv. 298.
[3] Marrier, 555; Pignot, iii. 3. He had been brought up as an oblate at Saint-Pons-de-Thomières, and when very young had been offered a bishopric. Pascal II disapproved and entered him at Cluny under Hugh.
[4] One of his few acts was to institute in 1109, on the Eve of All Souls' Day, a special commemoration of the dead of the Order and of their kindred who had died in the course of the year (Pignot, iii. 5, and iii. 30).
[5] These roused the ire of Bernard of Clairvaux (Migne, *Patr. Lat.*, lxxii. 915).

nave of the basilica; and at Cluny his successor Calixtus II was elected.[1] Calixtus spent Epiphany at Cluny, renewed its privileges,[2] and made Pons de Melgueil cardinal priest of Santa Cecilia. Very soon, however, some monks of Cluny had to protest before Calixtus against the extravagance of their Abbot; and there was scandal and dissension throughout the Order. Pons went to Rome to answer the charges, and finally, between pride and boredom, offered to resign his post. Calixtus accepted his resignation by receiving from Pons his pastoral staff, and in 1122 Pons departed on pilgrimage to Jerusalem.[3]

Pons was succeeded by the Prior of Marcigny, Hugh II, who ruled for only three months.[4] At his death the choice of the brethren fell upon Pierre Maurice de Montboissier, a great-nephew of Hugh of Semur, who had been brought up as an oblate at Sauxillange, and after making his profession at the age of seventeen, had lived as a Cluniac monk at Vézelay and Domène.[5]

From the beginning of his abbatiate Peter had to contend with opposition and dissension; and in 1125 this passed into a state of open war. Pons crossed the Alps, and finding that Peter was making a visitation of the Cluniac monasteries of Aquitaine, gathered together a little band of fugitive

[1] Calixtus was the first pope since Gregory VII who was not a monk.
[2] Marrier, 573. No bishop was to bless a church, consecrate the chrism, or ordain within the abbey bounds; its priests and parishioners might appear before no other tribunal than that of the Abbot and the Pope; and no abbot, bishop, or other master could lay hands on any monk, clerk or layman, freeman or serf, who had found asylum within the abbey bounds: only the excommunicate were to be driven out. The Pope advised the monks to regain 'by piety and charity' any rights of tithe that might have fallen into feudal hands, and ordered the bishops to give up any they might hold except for the expenses of visitation. No general interdict was to touch the abbeys and priories of the Order, but in such a case the monks were to celebrate their offices behind closed doors.
[3] For a full, if prejudiced, account of the proceedings see Ordericus Vitalis, *Historia Ecclesiastica*, iv. 386.
[4] Marrier, 583. All that is known of him is recorded in his epitaph: 'Here lies Hugh II, Abbot of Cluny, whose father was of Besançon and his mother of Lyons. Shining in piety, growing old in divine love, ever happy in worship, he was always thy servant, O Sovereign Creator. May he live with thee in peace, blessed through all eternity' (Pignot, iii. 45). The history of Marcigny (Dijon MS. fonds Baudot, 1018, p. 115) calls him a nephew of St. Hugh.
[5] Pignot, iii. 59. Many of his family entered religion. Raingarde his mother, niece of St. Hugh, entered Marcigny as a widow; and of her seven children who lived to grow up, Pons became Abbot of Vézelay, Jourdain Abbot of La Chaise-Dieu, Armand Prior of Cluny and later Abbot of Manglieu, Heraclius Canon and Archbishop of Lyons, and Peter Abbot of Cluny. Two of Raingarde's granddaughters entered Marcigny.

FIG. VI. CLUNY: THE SURVIVING TRANSEPT OF THE ABBEY
c. 1100

monks, unoccupied mercenaries, rogues and vagabonds, and made for Cluny. The Prior, Bernard d'Uxelles, who in his youth had been a soldier, shut the gates and prepared to defend the abbey. But Pons had succeeded in making himself popular within and without its walls; and knights of the neighbourhood joined with citizens of Cluny to break down the gates, while monks who supported his cause drove out Bernard and the few brethren who were faithful to Peter. Pons entered the abbey at the head of an unruly crowd of armed men, and all Cluny followed him; women rushed into the very cloister. Most of the monks who remained either supported Pons or were forced by threats and torture to swear homage to him; the few who refused were driven out or imprisoned. Pons seized all the treasures of the monastery—golden crosses and retables, candlesticks and censers, even chalices and reliquaries—and had them melted down to pay hired soldiers and to bribe the citizens. At their head he attacked the abbey's villages and granges, made himself their master, and installed his nominees. No monastic scruple restrained him: he acted as a brutal and violent feudal lord, burning, plundering, and slaying at his will. His war lasted without intermission from the beginning of Lent until the beginning of October.[1] At last, however, the Pope took action, and at the beginning of 1126 his legate summoned a synod at Lyons, and ordered Pons to appear before it. He refused, and he, the monks who supported him at Cluny and Souvigny, and the citizens of Cluny and all others who had aided or abetted him, or had taken or bought objects from the abbey treasures, were formally excommunicated.

The Pope himself then summoned Pons and Peter to come before him at Rome. They agreed to appear on the eve of Michaelmas, and exchanged hostages as guarantees in the presence of the legate. When Pons arrived in Rome, accompanied by monks and citizens of Cluny, he could not be admitted to the Pope's presence because he was excommunicate; and when the Pope sent cardinals to him to bid him repent, he declared that no one on earth had the power

---

[1] Pet. Ven. *de Mirac.* ii. 12; Marrier, 551; Ordericus Vitalis, *Historia Ecclesiastica*, iv. 425; *Chronicon Vosiense*, in Labbé, *Bibl. Nova*, ii. 301.

to excommunicate him, but only St. Peter in heaven. His supporters, however, refused to follow him in such a claim, and appearing as barefoot penitents confessed their sin and were absolved. Proof of Pons's earlier resignation of the abbatiate and of Peter's election was then duly made before the Pope and Curia, and a verdict was returned depriving Pons of every honour and every ecclesiastical function, and restoring Cluny, its monks, and its properties to Peter. Pons, still unrepentant, was thrown into prison, where he died of fever at the end of the same year.[1] Peter was restored to his abbatial throne, and peace once more reigned within the walls of Cluny.

Yet by reason of Pons's insurrection Peter's task was made doubly hard. He had first to rid himself of suspicion and distrust of, and among, the brethren, and to re-form them into a true community; and then he had little by little to make good the moral and material damage that Pons had done.[2] He made a gallant fight, but he fought a losing battle. He had to contend with dissatisfaction among the younger men: a novice ran away from Cluny, and made a great scandal in the town; a young monk, in protest against a petty penance, barricaded himself in the bell-tower and threatened to stone all who approached him until he was promised the remission of his penance and new robes. At Lihons-en-Santerre a rebellious monk who had been rebuked set fire to the store-house. At Charlieu the austere prior, William of Roanne, was poisoned by his own monks[3]; at Saint-Jean-d'Angély the Pope's aid had to be invoked to maintain discipline. Everywhere those who had supported Pons were ready to hinder Peter's work with calumny and ill will. Even his brother at Vézelay was arrogant and wanting in respect.[4]

In the Order itself discipline was relaxed, and there was a growing tendency for subject abbeys to endeavour to free

[1] Pignot, iii. 73. Out of respect to Cluny the Pope allowed him burial in the church of S. Andrea. Later his body was removed to Cluny, where Peter erected a tomb on which he was represented with bound feet, his right hand cut off, his left hand holding a broken crozier.
[2] Matthew, Prior of Saint-Martin-des-Champs, came to act for a time as Grand Prior (Marrier, 554).
[3] For the story of the appearance of his ghost to Peter the Venerable, see Pet. Ven. de Mirac. ii. 25; Marrier, 1323.   [4] Pignot, iii. 380.

themselves from its ties. As early as 1125 Peter had had to obtain from Honorius II a bull forbidding eighteen Cluniac houses to elect their Abbots without his consent,[1] and even so the Pope had to intervene to secure the submission of Vézelay, Saint-Gilles, Padilorone, Menat, and Saint-Bertin, not always successfully.

The financial resources of the abbey were seriously compromised. Pons had exhausted its reserves and wasted its treasures; but the daily needs of the monks increased with their number, and Peter was not the man to reduce the abbey's alms and charities. In 1130 he had to borrow a hundred and ten ounces of gold[2]; he had even to dispose of certain of the abbey properties. Towards the end of his life Souvigny was transferred to Vézelay, Charlieu to Cluses, Villars to the Archdeacon of Mâcon; a citizen of Mâcon lent ten livres on the town church of Cluny, another of Autun ten livres on the priory of Mesvres.[3] Finally the Pope himself had to intervene, and to order Peter to cancel these illegal contracts and to make no more. This would not have been possible but for the munificence of Henry of Winchester, who reorganized the abbey estates, drew up a fresh account of its revenues, for a whole year provided for the food of the monks, and acquitted the debts of the abbey. In all he gave them over seven thousand marks of silver.[4]

The property of Cluny and its dependencies was everywhere menaced. In the time of Pons the abbey had suffered considerably from the hostility of the Bishop of Mâcon[5]; Sauxillange had certain of its privileges usurped by the Count of Auvergne[6]; the abbey of Vézelay was at daggers drawn with the citizens, with the Count of Nevers, and with the Bishop of Autun. What wonder that Peter complained: 'Circumeo, satago, sollicitor, angor huc illucque distractus.'[7]

Yet Peter was not discouraged. Nothing could shake his personal dignity or his steadfastness of purpose. Those who lived with him could not but respect him; those who lived at a distance could not disregard the satiric force of his pen.

[1] Marrier, 1378.   [2] *Chartes et Diplômes*, liv. 209; Pignot, iii. 387.
[3] *Bull. Clun.* 65; Pignot, iii. 497.   [4] Marrier, 1624.
[5] Pignot, iii. 32. The roof of the nave fell in the year of Pons's invasion (1125) and had to be repaired at great cost.
[6] Ibid., iii. 357.   [7] Ibid., iii. 372.

He addressed to all the Priors of the Order a letter[1] calling them back to the observance of the Benedictine rule. He heard with horror that they ate meat like laymen:

'like hawks and vultures, they gathered wherever they saw smoke from a kitchen, wherever they smelt meat cooking. . . . Beans, cheese, eggs and fish disgusted them; they only found savoury the flesh-pots of Egypt. Roast or boiled pork, a well-fatted heifer, rabbit, hare, a goose chosen with care, chicken, in fact every kind of meat and fowl appears on the table of these holy monks. But soon such food in its turn ceases to be good enough; satiety brings fastidiousness; rare and royal luxuries must be provided. To-day a monk cannot stay his hunger but on the flesh of goats, of stags, of boars, of wild bear. Huntsmen, range the forests! Fowlers, catch partridges, pheasants, pigeons; let not the servant of God die of hunger. . . . Thou monk who eatest flesh, who sittest down to such banquets, is it thus that thou fulfillest the vow made before God at thy profession? Is this the promise made to thine abbot and thy brethren? Is this the rule by which thou shouldst live?'

Peter almost succeeded in bringing the Order back into the state in which Hugh had left it; but its dynamic force was exhausted and its potential growth was at an end. The great basilica was finished, and finally consecrated by Innocent II in 1131. In spite of a dreadful epidemic in the winter of 1144 Peter succeeded in bringing up the number of monks at Cluny to four hundred and sixty[2]; but such an increase was far from being a real advantage. The idea of the 'Benedictine family' had to be renounced,[3] and the Abbot could no longer control and influence his flock to the same degree.

In 1132 Peter decided that the time had come to draw up new statutes for the Order. The abbots and priors of all the Cluniac houses in France, England, and Italy were summoned to Cluny for the third Sunday in Lent, and two hundred priors and twelve hundred and twelve monks were assembled.[4] Peter proposed to restore certain fasts which were no longer observed, to restore the obligation of silence,

---

[1] *Epist.*, vi. 15; Marrier, 909.   [2] Marrier, 593.
[3] Butler, *Benedictine Monachism*, p. 210. The usual maximum for a Benedictine abbey was about seventy monks.
[4] Among them was Ordericus Vitalis, who has left an account of the assembly (*Historia Ecclesiastica*, v. 29).

FIG. VII. A CLUNIAC CHOIR: LA CHARITÉ-SUR-LOIRE
c. 1107

and to renew the ancient austerities of the rule. But many of those present were against such reforms, and pleaded that they were contrary to the traditions of Cluny, and that it was enough to follow these. Peter gave way on certain points, but carried through his reformed statutes in all their essentials: yet the new statutes were not uniformly followed, and in 1136 he had to get a letter from Innocent II giving him power to excommunicate those of his Order who did not accept them.[1] None the less, Peter endeavoured to make the organization of the Order yet more uniform, until his biographer could say that the daughter houses were as like to Cluny as the impression is to the seal that made it.[2] Yet the increase of the Order was definitely checked. It may have been partly due to the troubled state of Cluny itself that the great abbey of Reading, founded in 1121, and the abbey of Faversham, founded in 1146, though following the customs of Cluny, were not incorporated in the Order. Only four priories were founded in France in his time[3]; only one priory was added in Spain[4]; and the monks of the monastery of Santa Saba on the Aventine, given to him by Lucius II, refused to acknowledge Cluniac supremacy or to receive the Cluniac prior and monks whom Peter sent out to them. The former great benefactors of the abbey were nearly all dead. Only Roger of Sicily came forward to take their place.[5]

In the great world of politics Cluny likewise came to take a less prominent place. The political centre of France had definitely shifted to the north; the Order of Cluny was essentially Burgundian and of the south. In the north, moreover, the bishops had more influence than the monasteries; and though in the time of Peter the Venerable many bishops were of Cluniac origin, yet as a whole the bishops were

---

[1] Marrier, 1382.
[2] Ibid., 595. ' . . . Erat enim idem S. Martini Monasterium sub Cluniacensi Monasterio, in Ordinis, Religionis, ac fervoris proposito, pro modo suo ita consimile, et in tantum conforme, ut velut simulacrum cerae impressum, multis aliis ad Cluniacum pertinentibus Monasteriis, originalis sigilli imaginem familiarius repraesentet: et exceptis locorum distantiis, quae simul esse non possunt, non diversa, sed prorsus unum sint.'
[3] Dompierre, in the diocese of Amiens; Sainte-Marie-de-Montdidier; Clunizet; and the nunnery of Lavenne near Thiers.   [4] S. Vincente de Salamanca.
[5] Pignot, iii. 285, 315. Stephen of England gave Cluny the manor of Ledcumb in Berkshire, but he specifically asked that his monastery of Faversham should remain outside the Order.

hostile to Cluny.[1] Under Maiol, Odilo, and Hugh, Cluny and its abbots had taken a leading part in the great movements of the time; under Peter, leadership passed into other hands. Cluny had earlier done much for the success of the Burgundian crusades in Spain; but in the later crusades to Jerusalem the abbey played a passive part. The second crusade, it is true, was preached at Vézelay; but it was preached by Bernard of Clairvaux, the enemy of Cluny, in the absence of both the Abbot of Vézelay and the Abbot of Cluny.[2]

Hostility against Cluny was declared even within Benedictine monasticism. Cluny had owed much of its earlier importance to its gradual evolution into an Order, necessarily greater and more powerful than a single abbey. Such an evolution was its own peculiar creation; but it was soon imitated. New orders were founded—the Orders of Chartreux, of Prémontré, of Grandmont, of Cîteaux—that were able, unhampered by tradition, to modify and improve upon the organization of the Order of Cluny. The most powerful of these was the Cistercian Order, founded in 1098; and this was a Burgundian Order, a neighbour to Cluny, with houses in the very valley of the Grosne. Pons bequeathed to Peter a fatal heritage of animosity with the Cistercians[3]; and in 1124, just before Pons returned to Cluny as an invader, Bernard wrote his famous *Apologia*,[4] in which he defended Benedictinism as a whole from criticism directed against Cluny in particular; and then proceeded to an indictment of Cluny for its lapses from Benedictine perfection, none the less deadly for being prefaced by expressions of admiration and friendship for the Order.

The monks of Cîteaux had attacked the very customs of Cluny, so Bernard began by a half-hearted vindication of these. It is quite true, he says, that in several respects—in the

[1] See Valous, p. 313.

[2] Suger and Bernard both wrote to Peter later to try to obtain his support, but he replied that he was ill (Pignot, iii. 321).

[3] Pignot, iii. 94. The first cause of dissension between the two Orders was Robert of Châtillon, the nephew of St. Bernard, who had been dedicated from youth to Cluny, but as a boy entered Clairvaux. Pons sent the Grand Prior of Cluny to him, who painted to him such a picture of Cluny in comparison with Clairvaux, that he decided to transfer himself to that Order, to the great scandal of the Cistercians.

[4] The work was undertaken at the request of William, Abbot of Saint-Thierri-de-Rheims, a monastery that followed the Cluniac customs. He stayed for some time at the Cistercian Abbey of Clairvaux, and was struck by the contrast (Pignot, iii. 101).

FIG. VIII. A CLUNIAC CHURCH: PARAY-LE-MONIAL
c. 1100

use of fur pelisses, in the use of fat in cooking, in the number of dishes served, in the disuse of manual labour—the monks of Cluny do not follow the precepts of Benedict; but the kingdom of heaven is within. The Cluniac customs are intended as a way of salvation for the greatest number, and Benedictine austerities have been mitigated to make them more generally practicable. But no ancient customs justify the laxity that he sees everywhere: greed in food and drink, luxury in clothing and bedding, service, horses, and buildings. In every detail he finds luxury and abuse; and all this is due to the Superiors of the Order.

'They who should have shown us the way of life have become in their pride the blind who lead the blind. Where is their humility, when they walk proudly in the midst of an escort of many men, surrounded by a crowd of servants awaiting their orders? . . . A man would take them not for the fathers of monasteries, but for the lords of castles; not for the directors of souls, but for the princes of provinces.'

All Bernard's strictures were addressed against Pons and the lax usages he had introduced into the Order; but it was Peter who had to face them and to make such answer as he could. This answer [1] is dignified and restrained; Peter makes a curious quasi-legal use of biblical precedents to establish his points. He first makes a general defence against the allegations, striving to show that the Cluniac customs conform in letter as in spirit to the Benedictine Rule. Then he goes on to answer the counts of Bernard's indictment in detail: if they admit their novices before a year has elapsed, it is because they follow a greater exemplar than Benedict, Christ; if they readmit fugitive monks more than thrice, it is because there should be no limit to charity; if they neglect manual labour, it is because idleness may be as well avoided by prayer, reading, and other holy exercises. If they receive monks of other Orders, they do but do their duty to their neighbour; and if without their Abbots' consent, it is with Papal authorization. They have no Bishop: but they have the greatest Bishop of all, the Pope. They hold churches, and receive first-fruits and tithes; but priests have all these

[1] *Epist.*, i. 28; Marrier, 657.

things, so why should not monks? They own castles, villages, and servants, they receive interest and appear in law-courts; but why should they not receive the offerings of the faithful, and assume the responsibilities that arise therefrom? In details of diet and clothing, it must be remembered that the Benedictine Rule leaves some discretion to the Abbot; in the administration of an abbey like Cluny and in its dealings with guests certain modifications must be made because of its size and their number. Finally, Peter reminds the Cistercians that it is Charity, the fundamental virtue, which has caused any Cluniac modifications of the Benedictine Rule. Is it not this very Charity that the Cistercians lack?

Peter invariably addresses Bernard as an equal, a friend, and a man whom he holds in high honour; and indeed the quarrel was not personal between the two men, who, when it began, had never met. But the rivalry between the two Orders was very real, and the mutual hostility of their members very strong. Feeling continued to run high between them, and it was later embittered by the Cistercians, being exempted by the Pope from the payment of all tithes, for they held land which owed tithes to Cluniac abbeys.[1] Gradually and inevitably Cîteaux forged ahead of Cluny; in Spain[2] and in England it became the most powerful Order, in France the most influential. Such influence was always used in ways unfavourable to Cluny, and has done much to discredit the Cluniac Order not only for the twelfth century but also for succeeding ages.

When Peter died in 1157 it was not without reason that his brethren inscribed on his tomb:

'Dum Petrus moritur, pius abbas, jus sepelitur,
    Pax cadit, ordo jacet, flere morique placet.
Ille, salus patriae, mundi decus, arca sophiae,
    Nescius invidiae, vena fuit veniae.'[3]

[1] Pignot, iii. 117.
[2] For example under Thibaut de Champagne, King of Navarre 1234–53, S. Salvador de Leyve, given to Cluny by Ramiro the Great, passed to the Order of Cîteaux.
[3] Marrier, 602.

III

THE MONKS OF CLUNY

THE abbey of Cluny formed a little world, and in its microcosm nearly all the types of the greater world were represented: saints and criminals, men of action and men of contemplation, those who had hardly any experience of the world beyond the cloister, and those who knew it so well that they were weary of it, and sought a refuge from it within the abbey.

All ages, too, were represented. Men might make their profession when they felt death near; and according to the Benedictine Rule [1] parents were permitted to dedicate their children as oblates in the monastery. The parents brought the boy to the abbey,[2] and the chamberlain took off his childish clothes and dressed him in a linen shirt and a novice's habit. Then he came before the Abbot, and the formula of oblation [3] by his parents was drawn up, signed, read to those present, and handed to the Abbot. The child held a paten with a wafer and a chalice with water and wine, and wrapped his hand in the altar cloth, that he and the offering of the Mass might be received together. Then the Abbot blessed his cowl, put it on his head, and blessed him; and the boy entered the school.

Cluny was definitely not educational in its aim,[4] and under Hugh the number of such oblates was reduced to six. They had two or more masters to supervise them, and had no contact with the other monks, though they exchanged a bow of courtesy when they met. No boy was ever allowed to be alone, or to be alone with his master. After the monks'

---

[1] Cap. lix. [2] Albers, *Cons. Farf.*, 157; Migne, 741; Herrgot, 200.

[3] 'Ego frater N. offero Deo et sanctis ejus apostolis Petro et Paulo hunc puerum nomine N. vice parentum ejus cum oblatione in manu atque petitione, altaris palla manu ejus involuta, ad nomen sanctorum quorum his reliquiae continentur et domni abbatis N. praesentis, trado coram testibus regulariter permansurum, ita ut ab hac die non liceat illi collum de sub jugo excutere regulae; sed magis ejusdem regulae fideliter se cognoscat instituta debere servare, et Domino cum caeteris gratanti animo militare. Et ut haec petitio firma permaneat, manu mea subterfirmavi, testibusque tradidi roborandum.'

[4] By the time of Peter the Venerable, however, pupils were received for the school and boarded out in the town. Similar *externats* were established at Sauxillange, La Charité, and Saint-Martin-des-Champs (Pignot, ii. 414).

Chapter the boys had a chapter of their own, at which they accused themselves and each other of any error or infraction of discipline.[1] Their chief part in the life of the community was to sing in the choir, but they did not have to keep fasts so strictly as the monks or to sit through all the night services, but came in for part of the time, led by their masters, lantern in hand. If a boy was too sleepy to sing well at Nocturns, the master gave him a heavy book to hold to wake him up; if one was too young and frail to stand during the services, the master might give him leave to sit. In the cloister they sat against the wall with their masters opposite; no brother might pass between them. The monk Bernard concludes his account of their upbringing: 'difficile mihi videtur, ut ullus Regis filius majore diligentia nutriatur in palatio, quam puer quilibet parvulus in Cluniaco.'[2]

When the boy was fifteen, or later, if the Chapter decided that he was fit, he once more received the benediction of the Abbot and was admitted as a novice.[3] In the hostel of the novices the oblates joined others who had passed their youth outside the monastery: laymen of all ages, monks of other monasteries who had come to make a second profession at Cluny, and monks of Cluniac priories who had come to make their profession at the Mother House.[4] The arrival of would-be novices[5] at the abbey was announced to the Prior or his deputy, and to the brethren in Chapter. They were then brought into the Chapter, and the Abbot or his presiding deputy asked them, 'Quid dicitis?'—to which they made answer 'Dei misericordiam et vestram miserationem, vestramque societatem volumus habere'; and the Abbot replied 'Dominus det vobis societatem Electorum suorum.' Then they stood ranked two by two while the Abbot, according to Benedictine custom, told them how hard was the monastic way of life and how strict the Rule; and asking them if they were still steadfast in purpose, prayed, 'Dominus sic in vobis quod promittitis, perficiat, ut ad aeternam vitam pervenire mereamini.' Then the master of the novices led them into the church, where they waited until the Chapter

---

[1] Albers, Cons. Clun., 67.　　　　　　　　　　　　[2] Herrgot, 210..
[3] Certain deeds of oblation reserve the child the right of withholding his consent to becoming a monk after his noviciate (Pignot, ii, p. 381 note).
[4] These only spent one night in the hostel (Herrgot, 167).　　[5] Ibid., p. 164.

FIG. IX. CLUNIAC MONKS: GUNZO RELATING HIS DREAM TO ABBOT HUGH

was over. At the Mass, following after the litany, those who had not already entered the monastic life were led before the altar, and had the tonsure cut and their beards shaved off. Then the master of the novices took them to change their garments for the novice's habit, and they were shown their dormitory and refectory.

The greater part of their noviciate was spent in learning the ways of the monastery [1]—how and when to bow and genuflect, when to sit and when to stand, how to intone and chant, when to allow the hands out of the sleeves of the habit and when to cover them, how to ask pardon for lateness or other faults, how to dress and undress, how to use the monastic language of signs.[2] They were not admitted to the deliberations of the Chapter, but while it was held silently watched the food cooking in the kitchen. They were not allowed to read the lessons or to sing the anthem or the responses; they might not leave the cloister except in the processions of the great feast-days.

When the months of their noviciate were at an end, they came once more before the Abbot and renewed their petition to enter the Order. At Mass, after the Gospel, the novices came two by two before the altar, bearing in their hands the written act of their profession, vowing the Benedictine vows of *stabilitas loci, conversio morum,* and obedience to the Rule. The act was read and confirmed and laid upon the altar. They prostrated themselves three times, thrice repeating the versicle *Suscipe me secundum eloquium tuum, Domine.* The Abbot came forward, bearing his pastoral staff, and recited with the community the *Kyrie eleison, Pater Noster,* and *Miserere.* He blessed their cowls and put them on, and he and the brethren kissed them, and formally admitted them at the Chapter following.[3] For three days they wore their cowls day and night and kept dead silence; and then they took their part in the daily life of the community. For a time, however, they were everywhere followed by a *custos,* to see that their conduct was in every detail in accordance with the usages of Cluny.[4]

[1] Herrgot, 174; Migne, 702. Udalric says he will not presume to say, nor can he remember, how many and various are the things they have to learn.
[2] See p. 88. [3] Herrgot, 180.
[4] If a monk left the Order and returned to the world, the Rule ordained that he

H

Odo, the second Abbot of Cluny, is the type and exemplar of the true monk, for whom happiness was only possible within the cloister.[1] One Christmas Day, while he was still a weakly baby lying in a cradle, his father dedicated him to St. Martin and set him under the saint's guardianship. But as he grew up his strength increased, and, since he became a strong and handsome youth, his father ceased to give a priestly turn to his education and instead sent him to be initiated into the knightly arts of war and chase at the court of William the Pious. Yet his monastic bent was too strong to endure such a life.

'God', said Odo to his biographer, 'began to frighten me in dreams and to show me my life turning swiftly to evil. He changed all the pleasures of the chase into weariness for me; the more I took part in such diversions the more I returned overwhelmed with sadness and fatigue. About this time my father advised me to keep the Eves of the great festivals as he did himself. A few years later, after I had spent in this fashion a part of the night of Christmas Eve in prayer, it suddenly came into my mind to ask help from the Mother of Our Lord Jesus concerning my way of life. "O Lady and Mother of Mercy", I cried, "Thou who hast during this night given birth to the Saviour, deign to make intercession for me by thy prayers; I hide myself in the mystery of this glorious Birth. I tremble lest my life be displeasing to thy Son; and since it is through thee that He is made manifest to the world, may it be through thee that He may have mercy upon me." The rest of the night passed in prayer, in lauds, and in the solemn celebration of the Mass, and day dawned. The albs of the canons shone white in the choir. While the psalms proper for this solemn festival sounded in the chanting of the different voices, I—young and hot with impatience—sprang into the middle of the choir and began to chant with the clerks the praises of the King of this world. I should not have done it, I confess; but yet, when I recall the saying of King David, "Let all the nations praise the Lord, let all the peoples sing his praise", it seems to me that it was not with-

might be received back three times; at Cluny, however, such a monk was received back as often as the Abbot thought fit. He had to come to the Chapter naked and barefoot, and after his chastisement dressed and came back to ask pardon. This granted, he was taken for a time to live in solitary confinement until the Abbot absolved him (Albers, *Cons. Farf.*, 174).

[1] The chief sources for the life of Odo are the biographies by his disciple John of Salerno (Migne, *Patr. Lat.*, cxxxiii. 43; Marrier, 29) and by his monk Nalgold (Migne, cxxxiii. 86; Marrier, 16). He was of noble birth: his mother Adelaide was the granddaughter of Louis le Debonnaire.

out reason that I dared to act thus. At that moment I was seized by a violent headache, that overwhelmed me for a time and then departed. After the Gospel it returned worse than before, and if I had not propped myself with both arms against the wall I should certainly have fallen helpless and senseless on the pavement. The pain was so acute that with each spasm I felt as if I should die. This was in my sixteenth year, and for the next three years my head was torn by this pain like earth beneath the blade of a plough. They had to take me home again, where for two years they tried to cure me by all manner of remedies. But the more they tried, the less hope there seemed to be of a cure. One day my father, weighed down with sorrow and sighing deeply, told me the story of my infancy. "So", said he, "O blessed Martin, the gift which I offered thee willingly thou exactest from me to-day, as a pitiless creditor demands payment of a debt. Assuredly thou art most accessible to prayer, but hard to pay in business." Having lost all hope of regaining health, I saw no other course open to me than to take refuge with him, to take the tonsure, and voluntarily to devote myself to the service of him to whom I had once been vowed without my knowledge.'

So Odo took his vows as a canon at St. Martin of Tours, and Fulk the Red, Count of Anjou, bought him a prebend. For a time he there studied grammar, and then went to Paris to work at Music and Dialectic[1]; but he soon returned to Tours.

In 903 a Norman host under Heric and Haric appeared under the walls of Tours, and destroyed the basilica of St. Martin. For the first time Odo assumed an active role, encouraging the local peasants to help with the rebuilding of the church, and endeavouring, though with little success, to reform the Chapter, that had fallen on evil days in its morals as in its circumstances. We have seen how he gave up the task as hopeless, and set out with Adhegrin to find the monastic ideal at Baume.

In the history of Cluny he figures, in his maturity, as a great administrator and a great statesman. Like many saints, he united these qualities with a touching simplicity and a childlike happiness. His disciple, John of Salerno, reveals him as a precursor of St. Francis.

---

[1] *Vita Odonis*, Marrier 15.

'On his journeyings, if he found boys by the wayside, he would bid them sing, and as if to reward them for their play, would order them to be given something from his store, saying that they were worthy of no mean reward.[1] . . . In this and suchlike ways he compelled us to laughter, but his was a spiritual gaiety, and instilled an inner happiness into our hearts.'

His faith in his fellow-men was unbounded. Once, as he was on a journey, a young man came and threw himself at his feet, beseeching him to have pity upon him and to admit him to the monastic life. Odo bade him return on the morrow with some one who would serve as his surety. He came, accompanied by a lord of those parts. Odo questioned him as to the character of the young man. 'My father', he answered, 'this young man is the most remarkable thief I know.' 'Well,' said the Abbot, turning to him, 'first reform your ways, and then you may ask to serve your apprenticeship to monastic life.' 'If you refuse my petition to-day, my father, I shall hasten to my perdition, and God will demand from you an account of my soul.' The merciful Odo sent the young man to one of his monasteries, where he became a novice notable for obedience and industry. Soon he fell ill, and as he lay dying, asked to speak privately with Odo. To him he made confession and asked pardon for sins committed in secret: he had given a tunic belonging to the monastery to a poor man who was naked; and had stolen a rope from the cellar with which to gird himself as a check to his greed.

The charity of Odo was courteous and delicate. Once, on his way to Rome, he entered the city of Siena in a time of famine. He was at once surrounded by beggars; so the prudent John, who acted as his purse-bearer, knowing his master's unbounded charity and the smallness of their resources, withdrew, and went round outside the city walls to the Roman gate, while Odo, followed by the beggars, went through the city. As the Abbot crossed the square he saw three men by a window, of the burgess class, but in as wretched a state as the beggars. On their window-sill were jars of laurel-berries drying in the sun. Wishing to help them and to spare their pride, he approached the window

---

[1] Cf. the story of St. Bernard told much later by Jacques de Vitry (*Exempla*, ed. Crane, p. 120; G. G. Coulton, *Mediaeval Garner*, p. 61).

Fig. X. CLUNY: THE ABBEY GATEWAY

c. 1100

and, as if he really needed them, asked to be allowed to buy the laurel-berries, and named his own high price. Then he went on to meet his purse-bearer, who describes his coming

'at the head of a crowd of poor folk, like a man leading his troops to war. His joy was such that when I bowed to him as the custom is, he could scarce give me his blessing in return. Pretending not to know who these men were, I asked him what they wanted. "They are," he said, "the serving-men of God and our labourers; therefore hasten to pay them their wages." I distributed alms; and then, when I saw this quantity of laurel-berries, I asked him whence he had taken them and what he wished done with them; and then he answered us, in a rush of such gay words that I have never heard the like. He made us laugh till we cried and were past speech. Then when we were a little calmer, I besought him to free us from the burden of these berries and to give them back to those who had sold them. "No", said he, "for I should be afraid that they would then wish to repay us their price." '

No sordid circumstance could deter him from a charitable deed. Once in the Cottian Alps he gave an old beggar a ride on his horse, and himself bore the beggar's wallet filled with the crusts and fragments of stale garlic and onion that he had begged. It smelt so evil that John of Salerno moved away from Odo's side. 'Alas,' said Odo, 'this smell which seems so stinking to you, is the smell of the poor man's food; he bears the wallet, and you cannot endure even to see it; it is the very smell of poverty that you cannot endure.' Thus he went through life, head down and eyes on the ground, so bent as to earn the nickname of 'the Digger', but seeing only heavenly things.

Aymar, his successor, had no such power of leading men. His chief virtue was his humility; and even so he once gave way to pride. After he had resigned the abbatiate to Maiol he lived on at Cluny, old and blind, once more a brother among the brethren. One day when he was resting in the infirmary he sent one of the infirmary servants to the cellarer to ask for a cheese. The cellarer was busy, and refused, saying that he could not be at the beck and call of so many Abbots. Aymar, blind and helpless, was intolerably hurt; and the next morning bade his servant lead him to the Chapter. There he addressed the Abbot: 'Brother Maiol,

I have not made you Abbot over me so that you should per-
secute me; I have not chosen you that you should make me
feel the power of a master over a slave whom he has bought
in the market, but that you might have compassion on me as
a son to a father . . . I ask you, are you my monk?' 'I am,'
answered Maiol, 'I have never been more your monk than at
this moment.' 'Then if you are my monk, come down at
once from your chair and take the place which was yours
aforetime.' Maiol at once rose, and returned to his former
seat among the brethren. Aymar seated himself in the
Abbot's chair, accused the cellarer who had annoyed him,
made him bow before him, and gave him the penance he
thought fit; and then rose and ordered Maiol once more to
take his place.[1]

In many ways Odilo was the spiritual son of Odo.[2] Like
him, he had been a weakling as a baby. His limbs had been
so feeble that he could hardly walk; but one day his nurse
left him unattended before the door of a church dedicated
to the Virgin, and the child crawled up to the door of the
church, contrived to push it open, and to make his way,
'quasi quodam se manuum pedumque remigio fulciens', up
to the altar. There he seized hold of the altar cloth to try to
pull himself upright; and all his weakness left him. Like Odo,
he was a happy man. Jotsaldus tells us:

'With what joy did he advance among his brethren! With what an
air of festival did he take his seat in the sacred choir, casting his
eyes to right and to left over the plantation of youth that was
around him, remembering that verse of David, "Thy children like
olive plants about thy table". The more their number increased
the more openly did he show the joy in his soul. When this increase caused certain of the brethren to fear that it might prove too
heavy a charge, "Be not dismayed", he said, "at the increase of the
flock; He by whose will and voice they are called together will
know how to rule them by His providence and mercy." Thus he
became the father of a crowd of monks of all ages and conditions:
some still children, some youths; some in the prime of life, some
in old age; and although they came to him at different times, from
distant lands, with habits of their own, he knew how to unite
them into one community by the strength given by moderation

---

[1] Petri Damiani, *Epist.* ii. 14; Marrier, 270.
[2] His life was written by Peter Damian (Marrier, 316).

and prudence, by the love of a mother, and the care of a father, so that all seemed to have but one heart and one soul.'

Like Odo, he forgave much, and could see the good that existed even in the criminal. In 1012 the murderer of Stephen III, Bishop of Clermont, took refuge at Cluny. Odilo brought him to repentance and admitted him as a monk. When he proved himself learned and pious he even wished to admit him to priest's Orders; but Pope John XIX forbade it as contrary to canon law.

His deeds show him to have shared Odo's love for children. He cured the blindness of a child, son of a serf of the abbey's farm at Bésornay, whom he saw one day when he went into the farm kitchen to warm himself. Once, when he was travelling near Paris, he came upon the bodies of two children dead of cold and hunger; he had their grave dug, wrapped the bodies in his own cloak of serge and buried them, and did not go on his way until he had said the prayers for the dead over their grave. Sick people of every kind were brought to him. The servants of the Cluniac priory of Nantua one day found in the neighbouring woods a deserter from some feudal army who through terror and privation had lost his reason. He was brought to Odilo, who prayed with his brethren before the altar of St. Peter, and after the chanting of psalms and the saying of litanies, sprinkled the man with holy water and gave him one drop to drink. Not long afterwards he was restored to his right mind, and made his way to Cluny to give thanks to Odilo, bearing an offering of trout that he had caught in the blue lake of Nantua. The next year he came again, and followed Odilo as far as Souvigny.[1]

The great Abbot Hugh was another man curiously of the same stamp.[2] His mother had wished to bring him up as a scholar, since before his birth she had dedicated him as a priest; his father, wishing for an heir for his earthly possessions, destined him for the life of a feudal knight. So he brought him up to ride with boys of his own age, to manage

[1] Marrier, 326.
[2] His life was written by the Cluniac monks Gilon and Etzelon (L'Huillier, *Vie de Saint Hugues*, Appendix) and by Hildebert of Le Mans (Marrier, 414); by the monk Hugh (ibid., 44); and by his nephew Raynald, Abbot of Vézelay.

a horse, to wield spear and shield, and to become accustomed to plunder and rapine. But he was physically unfitted for such a life, too weak to bear arms, too sensitive to make war. He had nothing in common with the boys with whom he was to play; in every respect he fulfilled his mother's ideal of the budding priest. He committed parts of the scriptures to memory, and went often to church, but in secret, for he feared his father and knew he would call it laziness and waste of time. Finally, he was sent to study at Saint-Marcellès-Chalon and there, in spite of his father, took monastic vows.

What he did for the Cluniac Order has already been told. Hildebert tells us that it was hard to say whether he was more prudent or more simple; he never wasted a word, and never did an action that was not honourable. 'Ea plus patris habebat, quam judicis, plus misericordiae quam censurae.' His charity knew no bounds. His biographer tells us that he drank no wine, but ate a little food dry and fasting, 'as if to make mortar you should mix only chalk and sand', and that the rest of his pittance was served to the poor. On his journeys a crowd of beggars would gather round him, certain of receiving alms. He never refused audience, and never failed to give all his attention to the wants of those who came to him for help. Beside his bed might be seen a great heap of clothes of all kinds, that he and some of his brethren had cut out and sewn together for the poor. He had always a store of meat and bread and wine ready for the needy, that he might not add to their troubles by keeping them waiting. As a fisherman uses different bait for different fish, so did he bring men into the way of salvation by divers means. At Cluny in those days the lion lay down with the lamb. He went even beyond Odo and Odilo in the measure of his forgiveness. He forgave the murderers of his father and of his brother; 'nor was this all; the murderer of his brother, finding no place where he might find a refuge from the vengeance of his victim's kindred, found a noble protection in his bosom. Admitted to Cluny, he gained the life both of this world and the next. Hearkening to the exhortations of the Holy Abbot and touched with compunction, he put on the habit of a penitent, and so happily ended the

FIG. XI. A CLUNIAC GRANGE: BERZÉ-LA-VILLE. THE
ENTRANCE TO THE FARM

perilous pilgrimage of this world and only left this life for a better.' So gentle was Hugh's rule, so patient his discipline, that all men, whether proud or humble, eventually submitted to it. Count Guigo entered the monastery after a youth of luxury, and at first proved unwilling to renounce the comforts he had enjoyed from the cradle. The woollen robes chafed his skin, that was used to nothing but silk and soft marten furs. So one day he told Hugh that he could only bear monastic life if he might wear the clothes to which he was accustomed. Hugh consented, and by a special dispensation Guigo wore his robes of silk and fur beneath the monkish habit and cowl. But soon, living among his humbler brethren, he was ashamed of a cowardice in the spiritual life that he would not have shown in a knightly combat; and renouncing his privileges, he learned to mortify the flesh. But if Hugh could be gentle to the weaker brethren, he could be firm with those who sinned. Sometimes he had an intuition of such sin; once when he was visiting the Cluniac abbey of Saint-Jean-d'Angély he had a vision of the chapter-house at Cluny being struck by a thunderbolt, which he took to mean that his monastery was threatened with grave moral danger. At once he left Saint-Jean-d'Angély and travelled with all speed across France until he came to Cluny. There the priors could tell him of no unusual lapses among the brethren; so Hugh went away by himself and prayed, and then, coming into the Chapter, knew intuitively that one Peter was the sinner. Challenged, the monk confessed, repented, received his penance, and was absolved.

The little grange of Berzé was the favourite retreat of Hugh when illness or fatigue compelled him to retire for a time from the world of Cluny. He restored and enlarged its buildings and built a chapel, small and dignified, so that even if his administrative duties were suspended for a time, his duties of prayer and praise and meditation might still fitly continue. There, looking out upon the strange hills of Solutré that rise up like breaking waves, the old Abbot could meditate upon all he had seen and known: his home in the Brionnais, his school at Saint-Marcel, the recurring rhythm of the chanted Offices at Cluny; the beggars to whom he had given alms, the peasants and farmers of the Cluniac estates, the great flock of Cluniac brethren ever renewed as death depleted it, priors and abbots, bishops and popes, kings and emperors. He could imagine the basilica that was to be the greatest church in Christendom, and know that his masons were then toiling to make it fair; he could view the great Order of which it was the symbol, the Order that in all the lands of Western Christendom followed the rule and customs of the mother house; and full of thankfulness he could go into the lovely chapel of the grange, and for a space be alone with his God.

Many of the monks who led saintly lives at Cluny, less human than their great Abbot, seem to have cultivated austerity rather than grace in the spiritual life. The monk Benedict, for example, lived alone in the midst of the brethren, among them but not of them. Peter describes him: 'Corpus quippe attenuatum, facies macilenta, capilli incompti, ipsaque canitie venerandi, vultus demissus, oculi vix unquam patentes; os sine requie sacra verba ruminans . . . Silebat perpetuo, nisi cum eum certa et gravis causa loqui cogebat.'[1] His speech was ever brief, and devoid of any unnecessary words and graces. But if he spoke of spiritual things, it was always with sighs and tears. He was indefatigable in his chanting of the psalms and in his study of the scriptures, and always carried a part of the Bible and a Psalter with glosses about with him, so that if he came upon anything he did not understand he could look up its interpretation. He had as his oratory the little chapel of St. Michael hidden away in one of the towers of the abbey.[2] As he lay dying in the infirmary, he saw a crowd of figures in white raiment round his bed; and thinking they were the brethren, asked the brother who tended him, 'Brother Otger, since when has our Rule allowed the brethren to come here wearing albs? For so I see them to-day, in such wise as I have never heard of before.' 'But they are not here,' said Otger.—'I am amazed that you do not see this room and this house full of them. While you speak, they surround you on every side.' Then Otger understood that Benedict saw the

[1] De Mirac., i. 20; Marrier, 1278.
[2] The chapel still exists, see K. J. Conant, in Bulletin Monumental, lxxxvii, 1928.

Fig. XII. A CLUNIAC GRANGE: BERZÉ-LA-VILLE.
ST. HUGH'S CHAPEL

heavenly host, clad in white raiment, who had come to receive his soul.

If some were by nature destined, like Odo, for the life of the cloister, others, like his friend Adhegrin, were drawn to the lonely life of the hermit. In the time of Hugh there was a monk of Cluny named Anastasius who was irresistibly attracted to it.[1] A patrician of Venice, in his youth he had practised every austerity, and had finally set out to find a monastery where even Venice might be forgotten. He travelled across the Alps and across France, until at last he became a monk at Mont-Saint-Michel. There, however, he learnt that his Abbot was guilty of simony; and in horror at the sin retired to live as a hermit on a little island off the coast of Brittany. Hugh heard of him during one of his visitations of Brittany, and invited him to come to Cluny. There he continued fervent in asceticism: he would remain in the church lost in meditation when the brethren went to the refectory; he would kneel in prayer while others slept. Every Lent he retired to a cave in the hills to live for a time a life of solitude and privation.

When Gregory VII asked Hugh for a monk who would go to Spain to evangelize the Moors, the Abbot chose Anastasius. He travelled through the emirates of Toledo and Cordova, preaching the gospel and declaring that the Moslem faith made progress only by the sword, whereas Christendom made its way by charity and persuasion. But no one was converted: so he offered to undergo the ordeal of walking through fire to prove his faith. The Moors refused, for fear that he might succeed. In discouragement he shook the dust of Spain from his feet and came back to Cluny. Hugh took him with him on a visitation of Aquitaine; but at the sight of the Pyrenees he once more felt the call to a solitary life, and retired to live as a hermit on the mountains.

In the time of Peter the Venerable, when the community at Cluny was larger and the life there perhaps less happy, this vocation to a hermit's life was more often felt. One Gerard, who had been brought up as an oblate under St. Hugh and had proved himself a devoted son of Cluny alike

[1] Vita S. Anastasii, auctore Galtero, in Migne, *Patr. Lat.*, cxlix. 423.

in religious observance and monastic administration, was appointed by him Prior of Saint-Sauveur-de-Nevers. But he came back to Cluny to live on the top of a neighbouring hill 'whence, when the rounded clouds, heavy with rain, sank down into the valleys, he could see above them the Italian Alps, and a great part of France lying below'.[1] Here, lifted above the clouds, surrounded by dense forests, at the mercy of all the winds that blow, he found the peace and solitude his soul required. The Abbot permitted a few monks to join him, but the lack of water kept the numbers down. There, in prayer, study, and pious talk the rest of his life slipped away: 'curis omnibus mundi hujus exutus, tanto spiritualibus desideriis Deo fiebat propinquior, quanto ab humanis actionibus factus erat remotior.'

Similar colonies of hermit-monks arose round the chapels of Saint Radegunde, Saint Romain, Saint Vitale and Saint Jean. The novice Gislebert writes to Peter of Pithiviers:

'We dwell in the forests; a roof of leafage is more familiar to us than one of brick or stone. But our solitude is not like that of the swallow that dwells alone under the roof. It is not the density of the forest, but the remoteness from human society, that creates solitude. How then can we be solitary, we who since we came into the lonely places have drawn after us such a number of men, that our dwelling-place is more like a village than a hermitage?'[2]

To such colonies Abbot Peter used to come as an old man for rest and refreshment; but of the life of real solitude he did not approve. In a letter to a recluse[3] he warns him that solitude encourages pride, that leisure leads to laziness, that continual silence may later find compensation in chattering, that over-scanty resources may be the beginning of avarice. Moreover, the mind of a recluse is like a empty house in which all manner of ideas may find a lodging. 'Sometimes this great hermit imagines himself seated upon a throne judging men; sometimes he dons a bishop's mitre; sometimes he rules as Abbot over thousands of monks; there is no lofty position which he does not aspire to fill.' When boredom overtakes him, he first sleeps too long, and then seeks

---

[1] Pet. Ven., *de Mirac.*, i. 8; Marrier, 1258. The sight of the rose-flushed peak of Mont Blanc, seen thence, remote and almost translucent, with the plain of La Bresse below, is unforgettable.

[2] *Epist.*, iv. 33; Marrier, 863.　　　　　　　　[3] *Epist.*, i. 20; Marrier, 640.

distraction in contact with the world outside. Once his window is open, men crowd to him as to an oracle. He hears all their grievances, and talks them over; and unaccustomed words flow from his lips like water from a broken dyke. Those who come to him for confession, advice, and prayers will bring him gifts; and soon his poverty will be changed to riches, and he will begin to build. He will cast about for a site, dig foundations, hang his plumb-line, measure length and breadth. He may build a chapel or a bridge, but he will destroy himself; for, professing a solitary life, he will in truth live in the world.[1]

It is apparent that the eremitic life made its greatest appeal to those who had passed their youth in the cloister, and were weary of a common life. To those, however, who had lived longer in the world, the life of the monastery afforded not only spiritual solace but also the satisfaction of employing the administrative powers that they had developed in feudal life. A considerable number of feudal lords ended their days as monks of Cluny[2]; and a remarkable number of them held administrative offices at Cluny or her daughter houses. Guy II, Count of Mâcon, who as a young married man entered Cluny with thirty of his knights, while his wife and daughters and the wives of the knights took the veil at Marcigny, became Prior of Souvigny[3]; one Geoffrey, who had lived magnificently in the world, entered Cluny with his four children and became Prior of Marcigny.[4] Bernard of Uxelles, from being a great soldier, became Grand Prior of Cluny and lived to fight the usurping Pons.[5] Eudes Harpin,

---

[1] It is interesting to note the labours which Peter suggests as an alternative: planting trees, growing corn, copying the scriptures, making combs, and turning boxes and cups out of wood for the use of the brethren; and making rush mats and osier baskets.

[2] Casimir of Poland is said to have been a member of the community from 1034 until he was recalled to the throne of Poland in 1041.

[3] He afterwards, out of humility, resigned the office and came back to Cluny as one of the rank and file (Marrier, 459 and 1647).

[4] Ibid., 599.

[5] Peter the Venerable gratefully wrote his epitaph:

Egregius senior cui nil juvenile cohaesit,
  Bernardus Prior hac pausat humatus humo.
Hic post militiam coelestia castra subintrans,
  Consenuit, certans hoc in agone diu.
Iste sibi pro te numquam Cluniace pepercit,
  Huic sibi nulla dies absque labore fuit.

Viscount of Bourges, first went to fight the infidel in the
Holy Land and was captured by them, lived as a prisoner in
Baghdad, was ransomed by Alexis Comnenus, visited Constantinople and Rome; and finally entered Cluny. He was
soon appointed Prior of La Charité, and there, in what had
been his own country, he was able to employ in the service
of the monastery the local knowledge and local influence that
were his by feudal right.[1]

To join the Order of Cluny became for many lords the
crowning act of pilgrimage and crusade. Hugh II of Burgundy, Simon of Crépy, Eustace III of Boulogne, Bernard
Tumapaller, Count of Armagnac, all became monks of the
Order; until Gregory VII was forced to complain to the
Abbot of Cluny[2]: 'You have taken or you have received
in your peaceful retreat of Cluny, the Duke of Burgundy,
and thus have left a hundred thousand Christians without
a protector. . . . One finds enough, and almost anywhere,
of monks, priests and soldiers, and above all of poor God-
fearing folk; but in all the West one finds hardly any Princes
who fear and love the Lord.'

The greatest man who sought peace in old age as a monk of
Cluny came not from the camps and courts of feudalism, but
from the schools of Paris. Abelard[3] came to Cluny in 1140,
a weary and a broken man. Peter the Venerable had acted as
mediator between him and his pitiless critic, Bernard of
Clairvaux, and had encouraged him to write his Apology,
retracting those of his opinions that had been censured by
the Church and showing that he was guiltless of other
heresies that had been imputed to him. Peter then wrote to
Innocent II to assure him of this retractation, and to ask that
the ban of excommunication might be lifted, so that Abelard
might enter the monastery and end his days in peace. 'Let
no man', wrote Peter the Venerable, 'be permitted to drive
him from this house where he rejoices to have found, like

Sic bene totius pondus tolerando diei,
Nummum promeritum sero reportat ovans.
Huius vos fratres memores estote sepulti,
Nec cadat ex animo, quod tegat ossa solum.
(Marrier, 600.)

[1] Pignot, ii. 336.
[2] Mabillon, *Ann. Bened.*, v. 129; Petit, *Croisades bourguignonnes*, 263.
[3] On Abelard at Cluny see Marrier, 595, 850, 1354.

a swallow, a roof to shelter him, and like a dove, a nest where he may hide.'

For two years Abelard lived in peace at Cluny; and nowhere does Peter the Venerable show himself more nobly than in the description of him that he wrote for Heloïse.[1]

'I do not remember to have known a man whose appearance and bearing manifested such humility. Saint Germain cannot have seemed humbler or Saint Martin poorer. I set him among the first of this great flock of brethren; but by the carelessness of his apparel he seemed the least of all. When in our processions he walked before me with the community[2] I have often marvelled and been amazed that a man of so great and so famous a name should be able thus to despise himself and thus to abase himself. There are some who profess religion, who when they don the religious habit, do not find it splendid enough; but instead he was so sparing in his wants that, contented with a plain habit, he demanded nothing further. He maintained the same simplicity in his food and drink, and in every need of his body; and by word and deed condemned in himself and all men, 1 do not say only superfluities, but everything not absolutely necessary. He was continually reading, frequently at his prayers, and almost always silent; unless obliged to speak by friendly conversation with his brethren or by some discourse on holy things to the community. He offered the holy sacrifice of the immortal Lamb to God as often as might be, and after by my letters and labour he had been reinstated in the graces of the Holy See, he hardly missed a day. What more can I say? His mind, his speech, his actions, were ever meditated, and taught and bore witness to holiness, philosophy and learning. Such among us was this man, simple and righteous, fearing God and shunning evil; such among us for a little while, consecrating the last days of his life to God. For the sake of rest—for he was more than usually troubled with the itch and other weaknesses of the body—I sent him to Chalon, for the mildness of the climate, which is the best in our part of Burgundy; and to a

---

[1] He is equally broad-minded in the generous praise he awards to Heloïse herself. 'I had not passed the threshold of manhood ere I heard the renown, not of your present religious life, but of your noble and praiseworthy studies. I heard it told as a marvel that a woman still bound by the chains of the world was giving herself up heart and soul to the cultivation of letters, to the study of profane learning and useful arts. . . . By your passion for study you showed yourself to be above all other women, and indeed surpassing most men' (*Epist.*, iv. 21; Marrier, 850).

[2] This suggests that Abelard acted as a *magister* in the oblates' school. In the processions at Christmas and the other great feasts the *consuetudines* ordain 'tum subsequantur infantes cum magistris, deinde domnus abbas' (Albers, *Cons. Farf.*, p. 11).

home well fitted for him,[1] near the town, but yet with the Saône flowing between. There, as much as his infirmities permitted, returning to his former studies, he was ever bent over his books, nor —as we read of Gregory the Great—did he ever allow a moment to pass in which he was not either praying or reading, or writing or dictating. In the midst of such labours Death, the bearer of good tidings, found him: not, like so many, asleep, but awake. . . . All the monks of Saint-Marcel can tell you with what saintly devotion he made his profession of faith and confessed his sins; with what fervent love he received the holy viaticum, the pledge of eternal life, the body of our Redeemer; and with what trust he commended his body and soul to Him. . . . Venerable and beloved sister in Christ, he to whom you were first united by the bonds of the flesh and then by the stronger and more sacred bonds of divine love, he with whom and under whose guidance you have long served the Lord is now cherished in His bosom. . . . God keeps him for you, and when the day comes that He shall descend from Heaven to the voice of the archangel and the sound of the trumpet, He will restore him to you for ever.'[2]

Abelard was buried where he died in the Cluniac monastery of Saint-Marcel; but a few months later, at Heloïse's request, Peter had the body removed and brought it himself to her nunnery of the Paraclete. There he celebrated Mass for Abelard's soul, preached to the nuns, comforted Heloïse as best he could, and gave her the parchment with his seal to hang above Abelard's tomb:

'I Peter, Abbot of Cluny, who have received Peter Abelard into the monastic life, and have granted to Heloïse, Abbess, and the nuns of the Paraclete, his body, which has been secretly brought here, by the authority of Almighty God and all the saints I absolve him from his sins.'

---

[1] Saint-Marcel-lès-Chalon.
[2] Pet. Ven., *Epist.*, iv. 21, 22; Marrier, 850 et seqq.

IV

THE ADMINISTRATION OF THE ABBEY

THE free election of its Abbot was one of the chief rights of a Benedictine congregation; and, once elected, he became the father and the autocrat of the abbey. The procedure at the election of an abbot of Cluny is recorded in the *Consuetudines*.[1] The Prior and the brethren assembled in the chapter-house, and the Prior chanted the first seven psalms of the Gradual. Then, while the others knelt, he stood and prayed for the help and inspiration of the Holy Spirit.[2] When they were once more seated he bade them be assured of Divine grace, and the election proceeded, the elders giving their vote first. After the election the antiphon *Confirma hoc, Deus*, and the fifty-seventh psalm were sung, and the community passed into the church. After further prayers the election was declared, and a *Te Deum* sung; at the second verse the brethren came one by one to beg the forgiveness of the Abbot and to give him the kiss of peace.

The next day the Bishop was summoned to the abbey to confirm the election and bless the newly elected Abbot. The community assembled in the chapter-house. Thrice the

[1] The *Consuetudines* are preserved for us in the version written for Farfa in the time of Abbot Hugh (B. Albers, *Consuetudines Farfenses*, Stuttgart, 1900), the recension of Bernard, dating from about 1060 (Herrgot, *Vetus disciplina monastica*, 1726, pp. 33–364), and the version compiled about 1080 by Udalric for William, Abbot of Reichenau or Hirschau (Migne, *Patr. Lat.*, cxlix. 635; Albers, *Consuetudines Cluniacenses*, Monte Cassino, 1905). On these versions see *Histoire littéraire de la France*, viii, p. 391; Dom Berlière and Dom Ildefonse Schuster in *Revue Bénédictine*, xvii. 164–5; xxiv. 374–85; Dom Besse in *Revue Mabillon*, i, p. 15; and R. Graham, 'Life at Cluny in the eleventh century', in *Church Quarterly Review*, 1916, and *English Ecclesiastical Studies* 30. The account of the election will be found in Migne, 731. The election described is that of Hugh. The *Consuetudines* of Saint-Martial-de-Limoges published by C. de Lasteyrie (*L'Abbaye de Saint-Martial-de-Limoges*, Appendix XXI, p. 471) are based on those of Udalric.

[2] 'Adsumus, Domine sancte Spiritus; adsumus peccati quidem immanitate detenti, sed in nomine tuo specialiter aggregati; veni ad nos, et esto nobiscum, et dignare illabi in cordibus nostris; doce nos quid agamus, quo gradiamur; et ostende quid efficere debeamus, ut te auxiliante tibi in omnibus placere valeamus. Esto salus et suggestor et effector judiciorum nostrorum, qui solus cum Deo Patre, et ejus Filio nomen possides gloriosum. Non nos patiaris perturbatores eius justitiae, qui summam diligis aequitatem, ut in sinistrum nos non ignorantia trahat, non favor inflectat, non acceptio muneris vel personae corrumpat; sed junge nos tibi efficaciter solius tuae gratiae dono, ut simus in te unum, et in nullo deviemus a vero qualiter in nomine tuo collecti, sic in cunctis teneamus cum moderamine pietatis justitiam, ut et hic a te in nullo dissentiat sententia nostra, et in futuro pro bene gestis consequamur praemia aeterna. Amen.'

K

Bishop bade them by his episcopal authority, if any among them knew of aught that made the election illegal, to declare it forthwith. Then, the election being confirmed by those present, the antiphon and psalm repeated, they proceeded to the church. On the morrow the Abbot elect, wearing alb, stole, and cope, was led by two Abbots to kneel at the altar steps and to receive his consecration from the Bishop.[1]

Henceforward, wherever the Abbot went, he was received with reverence and respect.[2] Whenever a monk met him or passed him, he bowed low before him.[3] In the church, the officiating priest stood behind his throne; the censer was brought for him to bless it and insert the first grain of incense; the deacon came to kiss his hand before the Gospel, the precentor before the Oblation. The monk who came to receive the kiss of peace begged his pardon before and after receiving it. When he intoned an antiphon and bowed towards the altar, all the community bowed to him. He celebrated High Mass on the great feast-days: Easter, Whitsun, Christmas, the Feast of St. Peter and St. Paul, and the Assumption. On the other feasts he might celebrate himself, or appoint a deputy.

In the abbey itself the same ceremonial respect was maintained. Whoever gave anything into his hands, or received anything from them, kissed them. Even his messages were honoured; if when he was absent from the abbey he sent the community greetings or orders, the Chapter knelt to receive them. If any brother came uninvited to speak with the Abbot, he had to remain standing, and might not speak unless invited by word or gesture; and then had first to say *Benedicite* before proceeding with the business,[3] and again when he had leave to go.

In the dormitory[4] the Abbot's bed was in the middle, next the wall. He had to strike the signal for the brethren to rise; if by chance he slept late, so that the oblates got up before him, they were not to read aloud, as usual, but silently or under their breath, that they might not wake him. If the bell sounded to summon the community to the church,

---

[1] The full ritual is not given in the *Consuetudines* but will be found in the Roman Pontifical.

[2] Migne, 733.   [3] Herrgot, 137.

[4] Until a separate abbot's lodging was built, probably under Hugh.

the chapter-house, or the refectory, and the Abbot or his representative did not appear, it continued to be sounded until he came, that he might never seem to be late. If he came into the kitchen to warm himself, and found the brethren who were on duty there at their psalms, they were to be silent until he left the room. Whenever his name was read in his presence in chapter or refectory, all bowed to him. In any question of rule or usage, his word was law.

If a brother knew that the Abbot was angry with him, whenever he met him he prostrated himself and begged his pardon. When the Abbot entered the refectory two monks were waiting for him at the door, one with an ewer of water for his hands, the other with a towel to dry them. He sat at a high table on a dais, where he entertained distinguished guests. After nightfall a servant with a lantern accompanied him wherever he went. When he went on a journey the brethren who accompanied him kept near him, and sang with him the regular psalms. When they entered a city they lowered their cowls over their faces; but he might go bareheaded. By the time of Hugh, the Abbot was regularly accompanied on such journeys by a chaplain, an almoner, a chamberlain, and several brethren or servants.

When the Abbot returned to Cluny from Rome or from any other long journey, the community, vested in albs, came in procession to meet him; and after the next service he stood or sat with the brethren who had accompanied him at the door from the church into the cloister, and received a kiss of welcome from all the monks. At the next meal an extra course of fish was served in his honour.

The responsibility and power of the Abbot extended over all the abbey and its property, but he early had officers to help him. Under the first five abbots a provost nominated by them was charged with the supervision of the discipline of the monks, the cultivation of the abbey estates, and the maintenance of its feudal rights and dues. But under Hugh the growth of the abbey necessitated a more complex organization and a greater division of responsibility. The office of Grand Prior was instituted, as next in importance to that of the Abbot.[1] To appoint him the Abbot consulted the

[1] See Herrgot, 138.

elder monks, and then announced the appointment in Chapter. The Prior-elect was then led into the abbey church, to be solemnly blessed and prayed for by the Abbot.[1] In the Abbot's absence he acted for him, and occupied his seat at the high table; in his presence he sat in the first stall on the left in the choir, and at the head of the table on the Abbot's right in the refectory. The other officers of the community were under him, and referred to him for orders and advice. When he went on the abbey's business to one of its properties in the neighbourhood, he was accompanied by two of the brethren; if he went to a dependent house at a distance, he had two sumpter mules and an escort of three brethren, one of whom was in charge of his servants, his vestments and his other baggage. The vestments and the silver chalice that he took on his journeys were not his own, and as soon as he came back they had to be returned to the abbey's store, together with any money that remained from the sum allotted for the expenses of the journey.

The Benedictine Rule allowed the appointment of a monk of exemplary life as *decanus* to have rule over ten others. At Cluny this system was modified to meet the administration of the granges and manors of the abbey[2] near and far, which lacked the independent monastic organization of dependent priories. Each was provided with a refectory and dormitory, and generally with a chapel, cloister, and guest-room also; and over each a *decanus* was set, who, under the Grand Prior of Cluny, was responsible for the brethren and the farm. The *decanus* of every grange[3] within half a day's journey of

---

[1] 'Tuam, Clementissime Pater, omnipotentiam supplices deprecamur, ut effundere digneris super hunc famulum tuum, quem tuo servorumque tuorum servitio mancipamus spiritum sapientiae et intellectus, discretionisque dona in haec domo ita agere, et injunctum sibi officium ita administrare, ut et tibi placere valeat, et utilitatem servorum tuorum, te auxiliante, perfectissime expleat, propter quod et in futuro saeculo mercedem laborum suorum in consortio sanctorum tuorum a te piissimo largitore percipiat. Per Dominum, etc.'
'Domine Jesu Christe qui pie servientibus tibi munificus adjutor, et clemens retributor existis, hunc famulum tuum qui in haec domo tua nunc usque fideliter laboravit, et tibi servis tuis obediendo injunctum sibi te auxiliante administravit officium, pro laboribus suis solita pietate responde, et pius remunerator appare, et praesta ut in hac domo tua jugiter permaneat, et mercedem laborum suorum et hic et in retributione Justorum a te percipiat, largitoremque omnium bonorum se esse plenissima fide non dubitet.'   [2] See Map, fig. XIII.
[3] *Decanatus*, Fr. doyenné. The English equivalent 'deanery' has so different a connotation that it cannot be used. The *Consuetudines* give various rules of conduct

Cluny came every Saturday evening to the abbey before Vespers, to be shaved, to bring his linen to be washed, and to report to the Grand Prior. After harvest and vintage the Grand Prior went the round of the granges, checking the amounts of corn and wine in barn and cellar, and dividing both into two parts: one for the provisioning of the grange, and one for the abbey. In the time of Peter the Venerable a fresh *Dispositio rei familiaris* was drawn up to make better use of the produce of the granges. Each was made responsible for providing the abbey with bread, beans, and fat for a length of time proportionate to its size and fertility; some for a month, some for as little as a week.[1] This system remained in force for some years, but it did not make allowance enough for the suitability of the farms for special crops. It was therefore modified, so that Mazille, that grew more oats than corn, provided all the oats for visitors' horses at the abbey; Jully and Saint-Hippolyte had only to provide wine; and the other granges the bread, beans, and fat needed for the year.[2] Finally the *decanus* of Lourdon was put in charge of the supply of grain, and had to see that Cluny received 294 setiers of corn from his farm, 400 setiers of wheat from Chevignes and Péronne, and 500 setiers of rye from Montbertoud and Roman.[3] Mazille had to furnish enough oats for the horses of the guests of the abbey and the monks of the Order who came to Cluny for a single night; Écussolles had to provide 300 setiers of oats for the horses of the officers of the abbey; 200 setiers were received from

for the *decanus*: he is to ride with his cowl dropped low over his face, he is never to go beyond a walk, unless to bring help in case of urgency such as an assault or a fire; even when riding he is to sing the Regular Hours, and at the end dismount, lower his cowl, take off his riding-gloves, and ask pardon as if in the cloister. He must choose an elderly and discreet servant to accompany him; and the man who serves his table at the Grange must be decently dressed with boots and a robe, not merely in a shirt and drawers like an agricultural labourer. The *decanus* must be careful not to strike him for his faults and not to permit him to become too familiar in his conversation. If a woman comes to the deanery and asks hospitality in circumstances in which it cannot be refused, he must not sit at the same table with her or receive anything from her hands (Herrgot, p. 140).

[1] Pignot, iii. 388.

[2] Chaveyriat provided for September, Cluny for October and half November; Péronne for the second half; Écussolles for the first sixteen days of December; Chevignes from then until the end of January; Lourdon for February and March. The abbey bought its provisions for April, May, June, and half July; then Laizé provided for the rest of July, Berzé for three weeks of August, and Saint-Gengoux for the last week.   [3] Pignot, iii. 389.

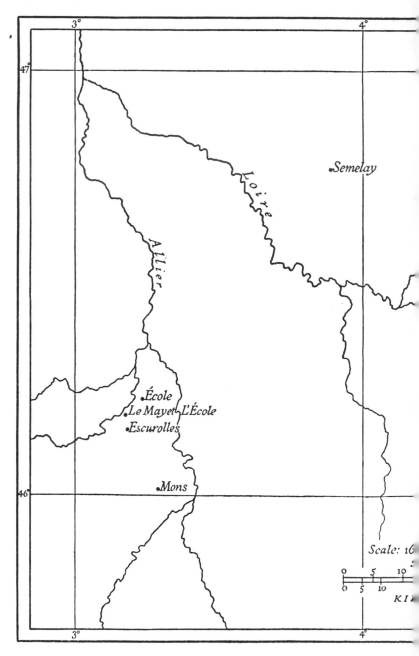

THE GRANGES OF THE ABBEY OF CLUNY

Not identified : ARPAYÉ EN BRESSE

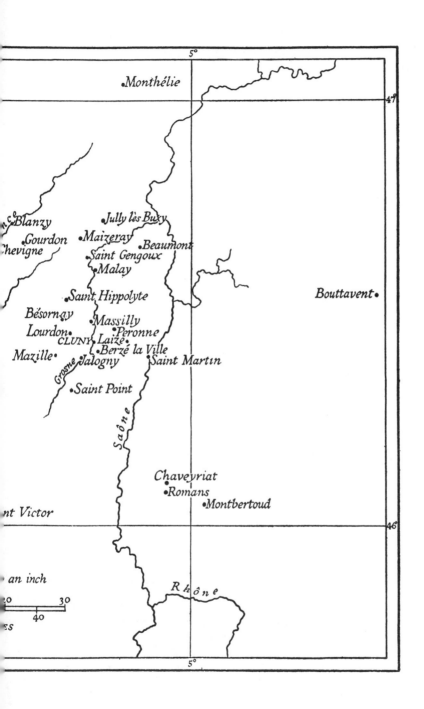

Monthélie

Blanzy   *Jully les Buxy*

Gourdon   *Maizeray*

hevigne   *Saint Gengoux*   *Beaumont*

         Malay

     Saint Hippolyte

Bésorngy   *Massilly*

Lourdon   *Peronne*

CLUNY *Laize*

Mazille   *Berzé la Ville*

Grosne *Jalogny*   *Saint Martin*

Saint Point

Bouttavent

Saône

Chaveyriat

Romans

Montbertoud

nt Victor

an inch

0   30

40

es

R h ô n e

Saint-Victor and Beaumont; and the rest had to be got from the market at Cluny.

While the Grand Prior was thus responsible for the abbey farms, the Claustral Prior took over the maintenance of discipline in the abbey. He never left the abbey, and acted as deputy for the Grand Prior in his absence. Each evening he had to stand at the door of the church to see that all came in in order, and duly dipped their fingers in the holy water, and duly bowed to the altar and the priest; and when the monks had gone to bed he had to go the rounds of the abbey, armed with a dark lantern, to see that all was in order: the schoolroom, the almonry, the kitchen, the refectory, the book-cupboard, the room of the novices; collecting anything left lying about, seeing that the doors were shut, that no one was in the cellar but the cellarer and his assistant, that all was well in the infirmary, that the chapel in the cloister was empty; casting the beam from his lantern round the dormitory; and at last putting it out and setting it beside his bed ready to his hand in case of need.[1] He was assisted in the supervision of the monastery by *circatores*, who went the rounds of the abbey at irregular hours to see that all was in order[2] and that the rule of silence was kept.

The next great officer of the abbey was the Chamberlain.[3] He received the money payments from the Cluniac estates that were too distant to send their produce in kind to the abbey, and returned a third part to the *decani* for the expenses of the farms. To him, too, were paid the annual *cens* that formed an important part of the abbey revenues,[4] and with few exceptions any gifts in money or kind. If the gift was ten sols or less, he handed it at once to the cellarer to provide some dainty for monks who were old or ill. He had a cowhouse in which any cows given to the abbey were kept; but oxen and sheep were at once sent to one of the granges. Hangings and altar cloths, gold and silver chalices, any other

---

[1] Herrgot, 141; Albers, *Cons. Farf.*, 146.   [2] Herrgot, 144.
[3] Migne, 751; Albers, *Cons. Farf.* 180; *Cons. Clun.* 4; Herrgot, 145.
[4] These were nearly all founded in the time of St. Hugh. The King of Spain sent 2,000 pieces of gold; and the King of England 100 marks of silver. Most of the revenues came from land dependent on the abbey: fifty sous from St. Pancras of Lewes, a silver mark from the priory of Linton, twenty marks from the manor of Offord, fifteen from the manor of Fobling, about fifty marks of silver from Padilorone, and various small sums from Provence.

gifts for use in the church were handed over to the sacristan. Otherwise everything paid or given to the abbey remained in his hands to meet current expenses and to form a reserve for times of famine. Those who could not give land or any richer gift sometimes gave an annual gift of a few sols a year; these sums he set aside for the repair of the pipes of the washing basins in the cloister.

When he bought or sold, according to the precept of St. Benedict he gave a little more and asked a little less than the market value. One of his chief expenses was the provision of clothes for every one in the abbey; each brother had a new habit and a new cowl for Christmas; a new fur pelisse every third Michaelmas [1]; and new shirts and drawers as they were needed. On Maundy Thursday the Chamberlain set out new shoes on four long poles in the chapter-house, and after the sermon distributed them to the brethren. Whenever talking was permitted in the cloister, he or his deputy had to be there in case any one wished to tell him of his need of anything; and all the officers of the abbey had to come to him for anything they needed—the cellarer for everything consumed in the refectory but bread, wine, vegetables, and condiments, and for these if his supplies ran out; the keeper of the guest-house for meat and anything his guests might need that the cellarer had not in his store; the keeper of the infirmary for his patients' needs; the *connestabulus* in charge of the horses for fodder and horseshoes; the gardener for seeds and tools; the Precentor for parchment; and the cooks for their cooking vessels.

The Cellarer [2] was appointed with the same ceremonial as the Prior. Each Saturday, in company with the Prior and the Chamberlain, or their deputies, he made a list of the fast-days and feast-days of the coming week, that he might know exactly what food would be required. He kept a record of the number of sheep and pigs at the neighbouring granges, and had certain meadows and fish-ponds under his charge, together with the abbey dairies, pigsties, and sheep-folds. Every morning early he went to the infirmary to find what diet the patients required. On Thursday and Sunday, when

---

[1] Herrgot, 146. Udalric says 'secundo anno'.
[2] Herrgot, 148; Migne, 761.

a course of fish was served, he went with the Prior to see
that every plate had an equal portion from the dish, and
that the dignitaries of the abbey were not given a larger and
better helping than the rest. He was responsible for admit-
ting the ailing to the infirmary, and for sending out notices
of the deaths of any of the brethren to the other Cluniac
houses.

The Cellarer had four officers under him: the keeper
of the granary, the keeper of the wine, the gardener, and
the brother in charge of the fish-ponds. The keeper of the
granary,[1] as soon as the harvest was over, received from
the Prior a list of the amount of corn gathered in from
each farm, and garnered it into his barns. He supervised
the bakery, which baked bread of two qualities, one for the
monks and the other for the servants. If the bakers did not
produce the due quantity of bread from the corn given them,
he brought them before the Prior and the cellarer for punishment.[2] He had to see that the right quantity of bread was
daily taken to the refectory, the guest-house, the infirmary,
and the almonry. He had to see that waffles [3] were made for
All Saints' Day, the feast of St. Peter and St. Paul, and other
great festivals, and that the due allowance of five each was
given out at supper. He had to provide little hot cakes [4] for
every Sunday, for every Thursday in Lent, and for every
'double' festival. For the five great feasts he had to have
plum cakes [5] made, a little one for every brother.

The keeper of the wine [6] was given by the Prior, after each
vintage, an account of the yield from the abbey vineyards,
and received from the cellarer all the wine that came in from
those in the neighbourhood. He made *pigmentum* or hypocras, which was served on feast-days, with some of the wine
mixed with honey and spices received from the Chamberlain.
He had herbs gathered and decoctions made from them, of
which some were served to the brethren from the day of
Saint Brice until Ash Wednesday, and others on Sundays
and Thursdays through Lent. He had water brought in for

---

[1] Herrgot, 150; Migne, 761.
[2] The usual punishment was a beating; but the servant beaten had the right to
claim a *solatium* of half a pound of bread and a cup of wine.
[3] *Nebla.*   [4] *Foliatas.*
[5] *Braciatos.* I follow the glosses of Herrgot.   [6] Herrgot, 151.

washing in time of drought, and was in charge of all the tuns and wine-barrels and their transport. He slept in the cellar with the Cellarer.

The gardener sent in his produce to the Cellarer, unless told to send it straight to the refectory.

The brother in charge of the fish-ponds had two special privileges: when he was bringing back fish he might ride in through the abbey gate and go straight to the fish-kitchen; and he might go out at night after Vespers to fetch in the fish from the pools.

Besides these officers who were responsible for the abbey's possessions, there were others who were in charge of certain parts of the abbey buildings.[1]   The keeper of the refectory, who had three brothers to assist him in his work, had to see to the laying of the tables and the measuring out of wine into the monks' cups. They set out the bread and cakes when they were served, and put mustard and vinegar by the dishes. If the loaves were burnt they tucked napkins under their chins, held the loaves against their chests, and scraped off the black with knives. They put fresh towels by the door twice a week, laid napkins on the tables, and on the great festivals laid table-cloths upon them. If hypocras was served on a feast day, the keeper of the refectory had to measure it out into small cups and to sound a bell.

The keeper of the infirmary[2] had his own kitchen and store-cupboard, with candles, fruit, pepper, cinnamon, ginger, and other spices, and dried herbs for medicinal use; the rest of the food for his patients was issued by the Cellarer. Each morning at the hour of Nocturns he went, lantern in hand, to see which of the patients felt well enough to get up; at dawn he and the Cellarer went the rounds of the others, to decide on their diet and treatment. He saw that their two meals were properly served, and that what was left of the food was not wasted; and at night, after Compline, he sprinkled the beds with holy water and saw that those who had been up during the day were in bed by the right time. He had two servants under him who slept in the infirmary, and were

---

[1] The *Consuetudines* of Saint-Martial-de-Limoges (Lasteyrie, p. 471) add a carpenter responsible for the repairing of the abbey roofs and woodwork, wine tuns, etc.
[2] Herrgot, 184.

summoned by a hand-bell; and a third who washed the linen, lighted the fires, and heated the water.

The keeper of the guest-house [1] had to receive the guests of the abbey who came on horseback, and their servants, and to see that they were well provided with food and drink, firing and candles. All letters that came to the abbey passed through his hands, to be given to the Abbot, or, if they were requests for prayers for the souls of brethren who had died, to be read in Chapter; and he kept the abbey's obituary roll. He kept the key of the cloister door, and closed it and the door of the church porch at night. In the morning, when the bell for opening them sounded, he came with clean hands and combed hair to open them and the door of the school-room. The horses of the abbey and its guests were under the care of the *connestabulus* of the abbey,[2] with two grooms under him—one for the Abbot's horses, and one for those of the Prior and other officers.

The pilgrims and guests who came to Cluny on foot were in the charge of the almoner,[3] who gave to each a pound of bread and a cup of wine a day. Besides such visitors, he had also under his care the eighteen almsmen of the abbey, who had a dormitory in the almonry and received each day a pound of bread, a cup of wine, and a portion of meat or vegetables. Every Easter each received nine ells of woollen cloth for a robe, and a pair of shoes at Christmas. Later, there were added to the eighteen three other almsmen, maintained in memory of Odilo, the Emperor Henry II, and Ferdinand of Castille. Each day twelve three-pound loaves of bread were distributed to the poor folk of Cluny who came to the almonry door; and once a week the almoner went through the town visiting the sick and poor, and taking them food. As he approached a house the women left it, that he might enter without breaking the Rule. He sent poor people out into the neighbouring water-meadows and marshes to collect rushes to strew the church and cloister for Christmas, Easter, Whitsun, Misdummer, the Assumption, and All Saints' Day, and paid them for their trouble in bread. He had under him a porter, a man to

---

[1] Herrgot, 152; Migne, 764.   [2] Herrgot, 157; Albers, *Cons. Farf.*, 176.
[3] Herrgot, 157; Migne, 765.

serve the pilgrims and almsmen, two to get wood, and two bakers.

The church itself was in the care of two officers: the precentor, who was responsible for the services, and the sacristan, who was responsible for the fabric and its contents. The precentor [1] was generally appointed from among those who had been brought up as oblates in the abbey, and from their childhood had been familiar with its ritual. He drew up the list of brothers to act as cantors, and to read in the refectory and Chapter. The whole ordinance of the services was his, subject only to the authority of the Abbot; but if he departed too far from traditional usage the matter might be brought up in Chapter. He had to set the pitch for chants and anthems, and, if the Abbot was absent, to give his responses and to read in his stead. If any one forgot his response, the precentor had to prompt him and supply it. He was responsible for the singing and reading of the oblates, and might chastise them if necessary. If a dying brother was to receive Extreme Unction, or if one died and was buried in the abbey, he had to see that the priest was properly vested and that all was done in due form; and he had to order the proper prayers for the souls of Cluniac brethren whose deaths were announced from dependent houses. For every service and occasion he had to see that the proper service-books were provided, and that every one sat in his proper place.

The sacristan [2] had charge of every offering made in the church itself by visitors and pilgrims: money, bread, eggs, cheese, or other offerings in kind. A tenth of the money and the bread went to the almoner; offerings in kind to the cellarer, and the rest to the maintenance of the vessels and vestments. He had control of a small revenue devoted to the purchase of candles, and besides those for use in the church, he bought them also for the schoolroom, refectory, infirmary, and guest-house, and for the use of the Abbot, Prior, and Chamberlain. Every Saturday night the sacristan had thoroughly to clean the church. The floor by the altar was washed, the pavement was swept, the candlesticks cleaned and fresh candles set, and all put ready for the celebration of

[1] Herrgot, 161; Migne, 748. He was also called *armarius* as he was in charge of the cupboard where the books were kept.   [2] Herrgot, 243.

the Masses on the morrow. He had the keys of the cup-
boards in which the sacred vessels were kept, and had
charge of the vestments and hangings of the church. On
festivals he started the ringing of the abbey bells. He was in
charge of the instrument that marked the time,[1] and checked
it by the course of the moon and stars, that the monastic day
might begin at the proper hour. He had a brother who
served under him for a week at a time, and a porter who
never left his post, but slept at night by the door of the
church.

One of his tasks was the preparation of wafers for the
sacrament on the eves of Christmas, Easter, and other great
festivals. The novices had earlier gone over the wheat, grain
by grain, to choose out the finest and cleanest. It had then
been washed, and sent in a special linen bag to the mill.
There the stones had been washed first, and the corn ground
by a lay brother, hooded and wearing an alb; and then the
meal had been passed through a special sieve before being
brought back to the sacristan. The Abbot appointed two
priests or deacons and a lay brother to help the sacristan.
They first washed their hands and combed their hair; and
then sang Lauds, Prime, the seven penitential psalms, and the
litany at the altar of St. Benedict. They then vested themselves in albs, and hoods that covered all their heads but the
eyes. The flour was cast into cold water, and kneaded on a
special kneading-table; and the paste put in an iron baking-
mould, which the lay brother held over the fire.[2] Mean-
while they all sang psalms or the Hours of the Virgin, or
kept an absolute silence.

The altar linen was washed ceremonially in church, every
spring and autumn, in great bronze vessels kept for the purpose. After the linen had soaked there in cold water all
night, it was taken to a room next the sacristy and was
washed with specially prepared lye and slightly stiffened
with a little corn-flour before being hung on a clean line

---

[1] *Horologium*; the exact meaning is uncertain. It may well have been a candle
marked with equal divisions for each hour. The text runs: 'primo horologium
dirigit et diligentius temperat, de quo, cum fieri possit ut aliquando fallatur, ipse
notare debet in cereo et in cursu stellarum vel etiam lunae.'
[2] An oven for this purpose can still be seen in the ruins of the Cluniac priory of
Castleacre. See Cranage, 71.

kept for the purpose. Finally, it was smoothed with a glass ball.

The most responsible charge of the sacristan was that of the relics which were kept in the church. On the festival of St. Maiol the monks bore them in procession to his church in the town, and the sacristan had to put them in a portable shrine, and to set out the candlesticks, the censer, the holy-water stoup, the three banners, and the bell carried in such a procession, with the vestments for the priests and deacons who took part in it. When they were vested the children of the choir came in in their albs; the Abbot sprinkled the relics with holy water; two men raised the shrine to their shoulders, and led by all the brethren bore it from the church, followed by the children and the lay brothers. The abbey bells pealed out, and at the cloister-gate the people of Cluny waited to join the procession and to do honour to the abbot-saint and the abbey in whose shelter they lived.

V

DAILY LIFE

THE Benedictine Rule, as modified by Benedict of Aniane from the precepts of Benedict of Nursia, was intended for the general use of all monasteries: 'et una cunctis generaliter posita observatur Regula, cunctaque monasteria ita ad formam unitatis redacta sunt . . . uniformis mensura in potu, in cibo, in vigiliis, in modulationibus cunctis observanda est tradita.' Its general precepts were indeed thus generally accepted,[1] but its particular prescriptions were commonly modified. The abbey of Baume had its own customs in psalmody and in other details of daily life, and these were inherited by Cluny.[2] Under its first four Abbots the life of the monastery was ruled by tradition, until its greatness made it a model for other monastic houses, and its traditions were reduced to writing for their benefit.[3] Through the study of these *Consuetudines* it is possible to reconstruct every detail of a Cluniac day of the time of Odilo and Hugh, when the greatness of the abbey was at its apogee and the prescriptions of the Rule were still strictly kept.

St. Benedict left a considerable discretion to the Abbot in the matter of the dress of his monks, according to the site and climate of the monastery, prescribing only that it should be of cheap local stuff. At Cluny, the monks wore a pair of drawers, socks, and a *stamineum* or long robe of wool, girt with a leathern belt. Above the robe was a scapular hanging down to the heels in front and behind, to which the cowl was attached. Above the scapular was worn the *frocus*, a kind of shoulder cape.[4] The upper garments were all of cheap black woollen stuff.[5] During the winter

---

[1] On the history of the rule see R. Graham, *English Ecclesiastical Studies*, p. 2.
[2] See Berlière in *Revue Bénédictine*, xxiii, 1906, p. 265. For a detailed account of the psalms added at Cluny to the Benedictine use see Migne, cxlix. 643 and 656.
[3] Berlière (op. cit., 262) considers that *consuetudines* were drawn up in most monasteries in the course of the tenth and eleventh centuries, but notes that the surviving texts are all Cluniac in origin. On them see p. 65 note 1.
[4] The novices wore a linen shirt and no scapular.
[5] Peter the Venerable, in his revised statutes of 1132, found it necessary to forbid the use of more expensive materials, and those of other colours, and the use of better furs.

a sheepskin pelisse and hood were added, to keep the monks warm through the long offices in the icy church. They each had two pairs of day shoes, a pair of winter night boots lined with fur, a lighter pair for summer use, and a pair of sheepskin gloves. Each year at Christmas the Chamberlain [1] gave each monk a new cowl and cape; new socks at Martinmas; new shoes on Maundy Thursday; and robes and drawers as they were needed. A monk was supposed to have two of each of his garments, three sheepskin pelisses, and five pairs of socks.[2]

The clothes were made by tailors working in the abbey workshop[3] or in the town. Each morning the brethren put any clothes which needed mending by the tailor into a chest in the chapter-house,[4] and shoes and socks in need of repair on the floor near by. The Chamberlain took them, had them mended, and put them back in the same place after Vespers.[5] If their shoes needed oiling, they first washed them in the conduit, and then gave them to the Chamberlain's assistant; or if they wished to oil them themselves, they did so in the kitchen before Prime or Tierce. When new clothes were issued, the owner wrote his name on them in ink, and sent them back to the tailors to have them marked in thread.[6] Every Tuesday, clothes to be washed were put into a chest in the cloister. While the monks were at Mass, the keeper of the granary admitted the launderers, and a monk kept a tally of the clothes they took away.[7] These came back on Saturday, and were distributed in the cloister after Nones under the supervision of a monk who saw that each man took the things marked with his name.[8]

Besides clothes, each monk owned writing tablets and a style, a wooden comb and its case, a housewife with needles and thread, and a knife in a sheath to cut up his food. The

---

[1] After Peter the Venerable revised the administration of the abbey the duty was given to the Prior. [2] Herrgot, 146.
[3] Albers, *Cons. Farf.*, i. 138. They had a long table to work at and another to sit on.
[4] Or in one of its arcades: the reading is uncertain.
[5] Migne, 753. [6] Herrgot, 146.
[7] Monks might, if they wished, wash some clothes themselves in the cloister at times when speaking was allowed (Albers, *Cons. Farf.*, 182; Herrgot, 214).
[8] If clothes or other property were left about, they were put behind the pulpit in the refectory. Any one who had lost anything got up in Chapter and looked there for it; and if he found it, asked pardon; and if he was a confirmed offender suffered some slight penalty.

brethren, according to Benedictine usage, were clean-shaven,[1] with a wide tonsure and a crown of hair above their ears.

The monastic day was not measured in hours as we know them, but in hours counted from the sunrise of each day. The landmarks of the day were the Regular Hours, which were sung in the abbey church.[2] These began with Matins at dawn, Prime an hour after, Tierce two hours later, Sext three hours later, Nones three hours after that, Vespers at sunset, Compline at nightfall, and Nocturns and Vigils in the course of the night. In the long winter nights, from 16 November until Easter, Nocturns were sung about two in the morning. In the other months, when the nights were short, Vigils were sung just before dawn, and the monks did not go to bed again before Matins, but instead had a short midday siesta.[3]

Udalric describes in his *Consuetudines* the abbey discipline for the Regular Hours. At the first sound of the bell ringing for Nocturns, the brethren raised themselves in bed and put on their habits, dressed without letting their naked limbs appear, folded back the bed-clothes[4] and went down to the church. Peter the Venerable[5] tells a story of brother Alger, who one night thought he heard the bell sound for Nocturns, and rose, and thinking that he saw the other beds in the dormitory empty hastened to the church. When he reached the lesser cloister he could no longer hear the bell, and thought he was so late that it had ceased to sound, since every one else was in church; and so he hurried the more. But when he reached the greater cloister it was not lit, as it should have been; and when he got to the church the doors that should have stood open were shut fast. So he set his ear to the door; but instead of psalm-singing there was a dead silence. Much puzzled, he came back to the dormitory,

---

[1] The monks were shaved once a week, sitting against the wall in the cloister. The razors were kept in a locked chest in the dormitory. The monks ordinarily bathed twice a year, before Christmas and Easter (Migne, 760). Bleeding was practised by one of the lay brethren; any monk might be bled when he wished, except in Lent, by leave of the Abbot, and was exempted from attending services and given extra food for three days afterwards (Herrgot, 212).

[2] They were also kept by monks wherever they might be, even riding on a journey (Albers, *Cons. Farf.*, 144).

[3] This was given up on October 1.

[4] The beds were stuffed with straw (renewed annually) with a hard pillow, a blanket, and a coverlet.　　　　　　　　[5] *de Mirac.*, i. 17.

Fig. XIV. A CLUNIAC CLOISTER: CARENNAC

and found it not empty as he expected, but full of sleeping men. So then he knew that it was all a dream, a temptation of the devil to wake him at the wrong hour, so that when the hour of Nocturns really sounded he should be fast asleep.

During the night Offices, for fear lest any of the brethren should go to sleep again during the psalms or prayers, one went round the choir with a wooden lantern in his hand. If he thought he saw a brother asleep, he held the lantern under his eyes; if he was mistaken, and the brother was only meditating, he bowed deeply to him in apology; if he were asleep he brought the light closer to his eyes to awaken him. If he had to do this three times to one brother in the course of his rounds, he left the lantern at his feet, and the sleeper had then to rouse himself and continue the rounds.[1] After Nocturns the monks returned to bed, undressing with the same attention to decency that they had shown on rising.[2] When the bell rang for Matins, they rose, dressed, and went to the cloister, where they washed their hands and faces, dried them on one of the three towels hung there, and combed their hair before going into church. They stood all through the psalms, but might sit one by one if they were tired. At the *gloria* of each psalm their hands had to be inside their sleeves to hold them up, that when they bowed very deeply in honour of the Divine Names their sleeves should not sweep the floor. When they bowed to the High Altar their hands had to be out of their sleeves, and their head had almost to touch the ground.[3] If one came in late he had to bow to the community, who bowed in return.

Before Vigils the seven penitential psalms and the fifteen psalms of the Gradual were sung, and after each of the canonical Hours two or three psalms for benefactors and friends of the abbey. Besides the Regular Hours a solemn Mass was sung after Prime and another after Tierce, usually for the dead, at which all the brethren but those who were ill had to be present. The chanting of psalms and liturgical prayers, together with hymns, canticles, responses and anthem on feast-days, thus took up a great part of the Cluniac day.[4]

[1] Migne, 706.   [2] Ibid.   [3] Ibid., 705.
[4] Peter Damian wrote to Abbot Hugh: 'The offices succeed each other with such

At the Masses the monks in the choir and the servants and lay brothers in the retro-choir came to the altar and offered wafers to be consecrated by the priest. On ordinary days only three monks were admitted to Communion and on Sundays five; the Cluniac usage[1] was to soak the wafer in the wine to avoid any risk of spilling the Sacred Blood. The rest of the community received in the refectory before the first meal the wafers which had been dedicated and blessed, which were called *eulogia*.

The morning Mass was preceded by litanies and prayers: one for kings and princes, one for the bishops and abbots of the Order, one for friends and benefactors, one for the kings of Spain, and one for any emergent occasion. At the second Mass there were prayers for the dead Popes, for friends and benefactors, for the brethren, for the kings of Spain, for the friends and kindred of the monks, for all who were buried at Cluny, and for the dead in general. Every Sunday, after the first Mass, the priest who was to celebrate the second blessed water and salt, asperged the pavement round the High Altar of the church and, accompanied by two lay brothers bearing a cross and a holy-water stoup, passed through the monastic buildings, blessing in the same fashion the cloisters, the infirmary, dormitory, refectory, kitchen, and cellar. The community awaited him in the little church of St. Mary, the chapel of the infirmary, and there intoned a collect, and repeated it in the refectory, and again in the Galilee, and between Easter and Whitsun at the great crucifix in the church.[2]

On Sundays the Abbot went after Mass with the children of the choir to wash the feet of the poor travellers in the abbey hostel. He himself gave two deniers as alms to those he served himself, and gave as much to each boy to give to those whose feet he washed.

At the five great feasts—Christmas, Easter, Ascension, St. Peter and St. Paul, and the Assumption—the brothers

rapidity that even in the long days of summer there remains only half an hour in which the brethren can talk in the cloister' (Marrier, 460).

[1] In spite of the prohibition of the Council of Clermont (Pignot, ii. 396). For a full account of the Cluniac Mass and Communion see Migne, cxlix. 716; Albers, *Cons. Farf.*, i. 4–136; Cabrol and Leclercq, col. 2084; and for a short résumé see Longueval, *Histoire de l'Église gallicane*, viii, p. 228. [2] Migne, 653.

went in procession round the cloister, bearing crosses and candles, gospel-books and reliquaries. Through Lent there were no miserere seats for the brethren to lean against. All reliquaries, crucifixes, and candelabra were veiled in linen cloths; and the gold frontal was taken from the altar, which was veiled in white.[1] On the Saturday before Palm Sunday[2] the relics were put in their portable shrines. A frontal of woven gold was put on the altar, and palm-branches were decked with flowers ready for the morrow. All the abbey bells were rung for Vespers. The next day after Tierce the Prior stood by the altar and blessed the palms, and the sacristans took them and gave one to the Abbot and to each of the brothers as they stood in their ranks in the choir. Then the long procession was formed, two by two, the monks, the servants, the oblates and their masters, the Priors and the Abbot, and after him the citizens; and with all the bells ringing went to the old abbey church of Saint-Pierre-le-Vieux, round the cloister, and back to the Galilee, where the palms were given back to the priest.

On Maundy Thursday the new fire was made to light the altar lamp, through a lens made of a beryl, and for three days was borne in the processions. On that day each monk washed the feet of a poor man, and gave him the pair of shoes he had just discarded.[3] Between Maundy Thursday and Easter Saturday no bell was rung, but a plank of wood was struck to summon the brethren to services and meals. On Good Friday they all came to Prime barefoot, and chanted the whole psalter. When the phrase 'They have parted my garments among them' was read, two brothers lifted away two cloths that had been laid upon the altar, in symbolic representation of the act.

On the Saturday night the brethren were busy preparing the church for Easter.[4] All the walls were hung with curtains of linen and wool, the benches were carpeted, and seats set in the choir. The night altar was adorned with its richest frontal, and on it were laid missal and gospel-books bound in gold studded with gems, a splendid crucifix and

[1] Albers, *Cons. Farf.*, 33. [2] Ibid., 43.
[3] Ibid., 49. New shoes were issued to the monks on Maundy Thursday. See p. 79. [4] Ibid., 54.

reliquaries. Before it a golden chandelier was hung from a rod and near it were set golden images of saints. Beside it stood the great Paschal candle, its wax inscribed with the year of grace and the epact. For the Mass all the hanging and standing candlesticks of the church were lit; fifteen before the altar, ten behind it, and fifteen above.[1]

On Rogation Day the brethren went in procession bare-foot, bearing crosses and reliquaries; and at the entrance to the church each received a staff with which to walk from one of the abbey servants.

On All Souls' Day they prayed, according to Odilo's in-stitution, for their dead.[2] For Christmas[3] the church was decorated as for Easter: 493 candles burned in the hang-ing chandeliers, and five great candelabra burned round the altar; a light shone in each corner of the cloister; and an extra light burned all night in the dormitory. At Candlemas half the church was adorned with hangings, twelve candelabra burned before the altar and five behind; on it were three golden chalices and two golden candlesticks. All the com-munity went in procession, bearing relics, holy water, censers, and candlesticks, and singing *O beata infantia*, to the Lady Chapel—the children first, then the brethren two by two, the Priors, the lay brethren, and last the Abbot with his pastoral staff. After prayers and the blessing of the candles, each brother was given one. The monks and lay brethren lit theirs from their neighbour's, the children from their master's. Then they bore the 'tabula' with figures of the Virgin and Child from the chapel into the cloister and thence by the Galilee into the church. There all, even the lay brethren, were vested in copes, and the children in tunics; and so they went to Mass.

With all this liturgical splendour, academic in its exact form, the services were yet in touch with daily life. In early August, when the grapes were beginning to ripen, the precentor presented some at the Mass before the canon, and they were blessed and afterwards eaten, as eulogies or un-

[1] Albers, *Cons. Farf.*, 57. Bernard of Clairvaux speaks of 'lustres like cart-wheels, girt all round with lamps, but no less brilliant with the precious stones that stud them' (Migne, *Patr. Lat.*, clxxii. 915).

[2] Albers, *Cons. Farf.*, 124.

[3] Ibid., 8; cf. Pet. Ven., *de Mirac.*, i. 15; Marrier, 500.

consecrated elements, in the refectory[1]; the new beans, bread, and wine were each year blessed and eaten in like manner.

Besides the 'Opus Dei' of prayer and psalmody, the brethren devoted some hours daily to scriptural and theological reading. On week-days, from Easter to October, they read between Tierce and Sext; and from October to Lent they read an hour a day. On Sundays they read all the time between the offices and meals. Each day a portion of the *Collationes*,[2] or lives of the saints of the desert by Cassian, was read aloud for a quarter of an hour after supper, when two meals were eaten, after Vespers, on fast-days when there was but one meal.

The Chapter was usually held after the morning Mass, in the chapter-house. In the time of Abbot Hugh this was forty-five feet long and thirty-four feet wide, lit by seven windows, with three rows of seats all round.[3] The Abbot presided, seated on his throne. Only the brethren had the right to be present, though the Abbot might exceptionally admit a distinguished stranger. After prayer and the reading of a chapter of the Benedictine Rule (whence the assembly took its name), or the giving of a homily on a feast-day,[4] the Chapter proceeded to business: the admission of novices, the expulsion of an unworthy monk, the punishment of sin, the exchange or leasing of properties, the borrowing of money, the acceptance of gifts, the reading of obituary rolls, and, exceptionally, the revision of the statutes. The monks were free to express their opinion on any matter, provided it was given with humility, but they might not argue with the Abbot; he in his turn had to listen to them and consider their views, but was free to act in opposition to them.

At the Chapter the Abbot accused the brethren of any public sin, and dealt with any secret fault that had been con-

---

[1] Migne, 750.

[2] Sometimes the homilies of the fathers or the works of Gregory the Great were substituted.

[3] Albers, *Cons. Farf.*, 137; L'Huillier, *Vie de Saint Hugues*, p. 629. The Cluniac chapter-houses generally opened out of the cloister: e.g. at Vézelay and Charlieu. At Beaulieu and Wenlock they adjoin the church.

[4] The surviving sermons of the Abbots of Cluny were for the most part composed for this purpose.

fessed to him privately. The culpable monk came in with his arms outside the sleeves of his woollen robe, ready to receive his punishment; when the moment for justice came, he rose and asked pardon once and once only; but each time a new accusation was brought he had to ask pardon afresh. If he was convicted of a venial sin the Abbot ordered him to be beaten with a rod. After his chastisement he had to remain prostrate before the altar during the services, shut out from participation in the rites, excluded from the common table, until one of the brothers came from the Abbot to whisper in his ear, 'You are absolved.' If his sin was more serious—drunkenness, anger, swearing, quarrelling, calumny, pride, envy, covetousness, the possession of private property, perjury, absence from the monastery precincts without leave, malingering, speech with a woman, or other grave dereliction of the Cluniac rule—the culprit had to stand at the chapter-house door barefoot, his scapular and cape off and folded under his left arm, his robe undone, a bundle of rods in his right hand. When allowed to approach, he laid his garment and the rods on the floor, and prostrated himself to ask pardon. Then he was chastised until the Abbot said, 'It is enough'; went out and put on his garments; returned and abased himself once more. When the Abbot bade him go, he went to the place assigned as his prison, where he remained alone. During the offices and regular hours he had to stand at the church door, his face hidden by his cowl, until the Psalms began, and then had to abase himself on the pavement until the last brother had left the church. He had to hear the two daily Masses from a corner of the chapter-house; and during the Chapter had once more to prostrate himself on the ground. The monk who brought his food might not speak to him; the culprit's only speech was with the brethren the Abbot sent to him to reason with him and exhort him. These, when they were assured of his penitence, asked pardon for him in Chapter. If it was granted, he was once more admitted, once more chastised, and after prostrating himself to ask pardon before each one of the brethren, was readmitted on sufferance to the community. He had the last place in church, refectory, and dormitory; he was not admitted to communion or to the kiss of peace; he was not

Fig. XV. A CLUNIAC CHAPTER-HOUSE: VÉZELAY

on the roster for reading aloud. He might, however, perform baser duties—act as cook, and wash the feet of the brethren. He had to ask pardon after every office and each daily Chapter; until finally, after an exhortation from the Abbot, he was reinstated. Then, lest any pride should be encouraged among the brethren who had not thus sinned, all bowed before him.

If a grave sin had been committed in the presence of laymen it was publicly punished, and the culprit was beaten in the open space before the narthex of the church. For a venial sin so committed the culprit had to stand barefoot and bareheaded at the door of the church on Sunday morning, when all the citizens came to church, with a servant standing beside him to answer their questions concerning his misdeeds.

Besides the 'Opus Dei' the Benedictine Rule prescribed manual labour for an average of seven hours a day, 'quia virtus est animae et corporis'. From Easter until the beginning of October all the brethren, except the old and infirm, were to work after Prime and before Vespers; from October to Lent before Nones; and in Lent for a longer spell between the third and tenth hours. Such work was generally agricultural labour.

At Cluny the ancient balance between spiritual and manual labour was changed: psalm-singing and prayer became the peculiar labour of the monks, who employed lay brethren, serfs, and servants for the cultivation of their lands. The necessary work of the monastery—the mending and washing of garments,[1] the cleaning of shoes, the baking of bread, and the cooking of food—were all allowed to count as manual labour, as was the claustral occupation of copying manuscripts. On the rare occasions that real manual labour was performed outside the cloister it was reduced to a ritual semblance.[2] Between Whitsun and November the Abbot, or the Prior in his absence, might order it to be performed on any day except a feast-day.[3] The bell was rung for Prime earlier than usual, the penitential and additional psalms were omitted, and after a shortened Chapter the dignitary who

---

[1] And even these were commonly performed by paid servants. See p. 79.
[2] Herrgot, 280. [3] Friday, a fast-day, was usually chosen.

was in charge announced to the brethren: 'Ad opera manuum ibimus in hortum', before he declared the Chapter over. Then the community proceeded in procession to the garden, singing the psalms that had been omitted at Prime: the children first, then the novices, then the brethren, and lastly the Prior. When they reached the garden they all turned to the east and bowed deeply; then the Prior or Abbot recited the *Deus in adjutorium meum*, and after the *Kyrie eleison*, *Pater noster*, and *Adjutorium nostrum* they bowed again, and recommencing their psalmody, began to work, generally, we are told, at weeding the beans. When the Prior thought it time to return to the abbey, he recalled them to him, and they returned in procession, still singing psalms, to wait outside the chapter-house and hear a short reading from the Scriptures or the Fathers commented by the Prior, followed by prayers and psalms like those that had preluded their labour. When they returned to work, as the Rule prescribed, after Nones, the Prior or his deputy summoned them from the bean-field after they had worked a little while, and bidding them sit in the shade of a tree, gave them a short homily, generally on the spiritual benefits of manual labour; after which they returned to their weeding and psalm-singing, until finally they all returned in procession to the abbey, to receive before Vespers an allowance of a drink made with honey, wormwood, and wine.

Another form of monastic discipline was the rule of silence. On ordinary weekdays speech was only permitted for half an hour in the morning after the Chapter, and for a shorter period after Sext.[1] Silence was kept all day on Sundays, on the great feast-days, and throughout Holy Week, Easter week, and Whitsun week.[2] Certain small tasks —washing wine-cups, sharpening knives, washing and drying clothes—could only be performed at times when speech was permitted. When at other times it was absolutely necessary to communicate with another, a language of signs was used of great fullness and elaboration.[3] For bread (since

---

[1] Peter the Venerable suppressed the second period. The brethren might call nothing 'mine' but their father and mother: everything else was 'ours'. Monks had to be spoken of as 'Dominus frater N.'
[2] Peter the Venerable prescribed it for the whole of Lent.
[3] Migne, 703; Herrgot, 169.

it is round) the thumbs and first fingers of both hands were bent in a circle; for beans, the tip of the first finger was put on the first joint of the thumb; for eggs, one finger was knocked on another as one knocks an egg-shell to break it; for vegetables, one finger was knocked on another as if cutting them up; for fish, the hand was moved like a fish's tail; for pancakes, the hair was ruffled; for cheese, the two hands were pressed obliquely together. Such signs could be combined to give new meanings; for a cheese-tart the signs for bread and cheese were given, and then one hand was hollowed tart-fashion; for waffles, the bread sign was given, and then a finger was waved to show their indentations. There were special signs for every kind of fish, fruit, vegetable, and drink; for all the vessels used in the kitchen and refectory; for all garments and bed-clothes, for needles, combs, and knives, for all the church services and their parts, for the different kinds of service-books, for monks, clerks, laymen, and all the officers of the abbey; for speaking, hearing, knowing and not knowing, understanding, dressing, undressing, and washing; for good and bad; for past and present; for fast and slow: a strange monastic language in which all the necessities of monastic life could be expressed.

The Benedictine Rule prescribed abstinence from meat, except in case of illness, and limited the allowance of food. Its precepts seem to have been strictly followed at Cluny in the days of the abbey's splendour. Two meals a day were ordinarily served: dinner and supper. The first consisted of three courses: a dish of dried beans, a course of cheese or eggs,[1] replaced by fish[2] on Thursdays, Sundays, and feast-days, and a third of whatever vegetables the monastery garden provided at that season. On the great feast-days onions and little cakes were served instead of beans. The vegetables were cooked with fat, except on Ember Days and during Lent,[3] and were seasoned with salt. Pepper was

[1] Bernard of Clairvaux (Migne, *Patr. Lat.* clxxii. 914), suggests that these were cooked with care: 'Who may tell of the eggs alone, in how many ways they are tossed and vexed, how busily they are turned and turned again, beaten to froth or hard-boiled and minced, now fried and now baked, now stuffed and now mixed or again brought up one by one?' (trans. Coulton, *Mediaeval Garner*, 69).

[2] William, Count of Ponthieu and Montreuil, endowed Cluny with an annual allowance of ten thousand herrings, and Count Eustace of Boulogne with twenty thousand more (Pignot, iii. 384).   [3] Migne, 726.

allowed when the beans were green and unappetizing.[1] The daily allowance of bread was about a pound, but if a monk had eaten it all at dinner, he was allowed another half-pound for supper.

The vegetables were cooked in the monks' kitchen,[2] *coquina regularis*, by the four monks [3] who were on duty for the week;[4] the fish and eggs were cooked in a different kitchen by the abbey servants. The *Consuetudines* [5] give exact instructions for the kitchen utensils—three great cooking-pots, one for the beans, one for other vegetables, one on three legs for lye; four large bowls, one kept for half-cooked beans, one to stand under the water-faucet for washing vegetables, one for washing-up, and one to hold the hot water sent up for the brothers to shave with; three great cooking-spoons, one for stirring beans, one for other vegetables, one for fat; a shovel; a pair of tongs; four pairs of cooking-sleeves; two hand-screens to protect the cooks from the heat of the flames; three cloths, clean every Thursday; a knife for lard, and a stone to sharpen it with; a saucepan for heating water and melting fat; a skimmer for fat; a salt-cellar and spice-box; a pail for water; two brooms; two netted dish-cloths; two saucepan-boards; two stools; a stand for the vegetable bowl; a stone base on which to set the hot cooking-pots; a pair of bellows and a wicker fan; two pot-hooks; a washing-trough, and two pulleys to move the vessels for hot water from the faucet to the fire. The *Consuetudines* also give instructions how the cooks are to take off their capes and hang them up outside the kitchen, how they are to wash and soak the beans and put them in the cooking-pots with water, how they are to skim and watch the pots, how they are to take them off the fire as soon as the skins of the beans crack, and add salt and fat; how they are to clean the pots and to use them to heat the water for washing-up, and finally to set them to drain on a sloping board; how

---

[1] If it was used the beans were cooked in the other kitchen.
[2] At Maillezais there remains a hexagonal kitchen with a central hearth, while at Menat there is a rather later kitchen of rectangular shape. (Fig. XVI.)
[3] Migne, 726; Herrgot, 236, says six.
[4] Even the Abbot had to take his turn at this service, which Benedict especially recommends as encouraging humility and charity.
[5] Migne, 726.

Fig. XVI. A CLUNIAC KITCHEN: MOZAT

they are to cover the fire at night to keep it in, and sweep and clean the kitchen on Saturdays: and how through these operations prayers are to be recited and as far as may be the Hours kept. The cooks attended Mass, leaving the vegetables on a slow fire with more water in the pot than usual, and a lay brother to watch them.

From Easter to Whitsun the monks dined at midday, and supped at sunset; on Wednesdays from Whitsun to September, to commemorate the Betrayal of our Lord, dinner was not till after Nones, about three in the afternoon. From the middle of September until Lent, dinner was always at this hour, and supper was not served except on Sundays and feast-days, and in the octaves of St. Martin, Christmas, and the Epiphany. During Lent only one meal was served, and that at sunset; on Good Friday it consisted of dry bread and uncooked vegetables. If when meal-time came any of the dishes was not ready, the cellarer removed the clapper of the refectory bell, and the brethren remained in the choir while one of them read aloud until all was prepared.

The children and young novices, any brethren engaged in heavy work, the cooks for the week, the reader in the refectory—and the whole community when the offices were very long—were regaled in the middle of the morning with a quarter of a pound of bread and a little wine, known as *mistum*. St. Benedict left the use of wine to the discretion of the Abbot, though setting a limit [1] to the amount permissible. At Cluny, lying among the vineyards of the Beaujolais and Mâconnais, it was the natural drink, and a cup—called *justitia*, from the phrase *poculum justitiae*—was allowed to each monk daily. A small quantity of hypocras was served on feast-days,[2] and decoctions of herbs were given in the winter and during Lent. During the summer the monks were allowed to come to the refectory to quench their thirst after Nones, or on fast-days after Vespers. Each cup was set out in the summer covered with a little sprig of box to keep off the flies, and a twig of vine dipped in glue was set beside each place as a fly-trap, and renewed every other day.

---

[1] About eighteen fluid ounces, according to Mabillon.
[2] Peter the Venerable endeavoured to suppress the usage for every day but Maundy Thursday.

All meals were served in the refectory. Originally this was ninety feet long and twenty-five feet wide, lit by twenty-two windows five feet high,[1] but Abbot Hugh rebuilt it on a yet larger scale, with a width of sixty feet and a length of a hundred.[2] Its walls were adorned with paintings of scenes from the Old and New Testaments and of the founders and benefactors of the abbey, an immense figure of Christ in Majesty, and a scene of the Last Judgement with the inscription:

> 'Ecce dies magnus, quo judex praesidet agnus,
> Sponte vel ingratum cui subditur omne creatum.
> Infelix vere cui non datur ista timere!
> Nam praesens ignis domus est aeterna malignis.
> Deo Gratias.'

Six tables were set lengthwise in the body of the hall, and three on the dais at the top—the Grand Prior's to the right, the Claustral Prior's to the left, and the Abbot's in the middle. The brethren washed their hands in the cloister before coming in. Every one stood until the Abbot entered and took his place at the High Table. No one began to eat until the *eulogia* had been distributed and the lector had begun to read. At the end of the meal each brother collected his crumbs into a little heap with his knife, and they were swept up with a fan into a dish. After dinner the monks either sat for a short time in the cloister reading, or, if they preferred, read lying on their beds.

Besides the food for the community, meat and drink had also to be provided for the guests and almsmen of the abbey. Guests who came on horseback to the abbey were received without question for three days in the guest-house,[3] which contained separate lodgings for forty men and thirty women and a common refectory. There was a guest-master to look after them, with a cook, porter, groom, and other servants under him.

When the guest arrived he was conducted to the church

---

[1] Albers, *Cons. Farf.*, 137.

[2] Marrier, 1639. An eighteenth-century description says that it was very high and had aisles like a church. Philippe Bouché (Bib. Nat. MS. nouv. acq. franç. 4336) quotes a seventeenth-century account which confirms this, and adds that it had about thirty-six windows. Remains of an early thirteenth-century refectory survive in the Cluniac priory of Ganagobie. (Fig. XVII 8.) [3] Albers, *Cons. Farf.*, 138.

Fig. XVII. THE RUINS OF A CLUNIAC REFECTORY: GANAGOBIE

by the Abbot or his deputy, and taken to the guest-house. Later the visitor (having taken off his noisy riding-boots and spurs) was allowed to visit the almonry, cellars, kitchen, refectory, novice-chamber, dormitory,[1] and infirmary of the abbey at a time when the monks were in church. The guest-master got what provisions he needed from the cellarer, and himself drew as much wine as was required. The guests' horses were tended and fed by the abbey *connestabulus*,[2] who provided the guests with any horseshoes they needed. If the visitor were a monk of another order he was shown the ways of the monastery; if he were an Abbot he sat at the high table beside the Abbot of Cluny, and took an honourable part in the services. A Bishop or other great personage was escorted in procession to the church, and thence to the refectory, where the Abbot or Prior poured water over his hands. Poor priests were invited to dine in the abbey refectory; nuns, who might not enter the abbey, were given bread and wine at the abbey gate.

The visitors to the abbey who came afoot, but were not of the class that went to the almonry, were lodged in the town, and were provided by the guest-master with bread and wine, and, if they were not too numerous, with meat also.[3]

The poor pilgrims[4] were received at the almonry, which was maintained by a tenth of all moneys offered in the church and a tenth of all tithes paid in money. Besides these funds, the almoner drew a full allowance of food and wine for thirty days on the death of any monk of the Cluniac Order, wherever he died.[5] The almoner also received the three portions which were daily set on the High Table in

---

[1] In the time of Hugh the dormitory was 160 feet long by thirty-four feet broad. It was twenty-three feet high and was lit by ninety-seven windows two and a half feet wide and as high as a man with his arms stretched upwards. Near it were the baths and the latrines, seventy by twenty-three feet, with forty-five conveniences, each with a little window above (Albers, op. cit., 137). The drainage appears to have been by a conduit running into the Grosne. (Cf. the 120 separate conveniences, one for each monk, in the Cluniac monastery of Lewes. Prior, *Gothic Art in England*, p. 44.) The men's and women's quarters in the guest-house, the infirmary and the novices' quarters each had their separate latrines, with a separate convenience for each inhabitant.

[2] Migne, 764. There was a stable with stalls, and a solar for the servants (Albers, loc. cit.).   [3] Albers, *Cons. Farf.*, 177.

[4] Those who came to Cluny for markets, fairs, or lawsuits were not received.

[5] Peter the Venerable, owing to the increasing numbers, limited these allowances to fifty a day.

memory of Abbot Odilo, the Emperor Henry II, and the King of Spain; and the broken meats from the monks' table. Each pilgrim was allowed a pound of bread the first day, half a pound the second, and half a monk's measure of wine. If any of them had left a weary or ailing wife or friend at his lodgings in the town, he was given an allowance to take to them. Each day the almoner was given twelve cakes of three pounds' weight to give to the old and ailing. Each day three brethren came to the almonry after dinner, and solemnly washed the feet of three poor men, and gave them a gift of bread and wine. On Quinquagesima Sunday all the poor who chose to come were regaled with a meal of as much salt pork as they could eat; Udalric, writing about 1085, declares that in the current year seventeen thousand persons came and two hundred and fifty hogs were eaten.[1] On Maundy Thursday as many poor men as there were brethren were given a meal of beans and millet, and had their feet washed by the monks; afterwards they were each given a cup of wine and two deniers. At Whitsun the same number were fed with bread, meat, and wine; and bread and wine were again freely given on the Monday after Trinity Sunday.

The remaining kitchen in the abbey was attached to the infirmary, where more delicate food suitable for invalids was cooked. If a monk felt too ill to continue the daily round he asked pardon in Chapter: 'Infirmus sum, et non possum sequi Conventum.'[2] He was then given extra food, and a place apart from the rest in church, so that he might sit during the services if he wished. If he were not better in two or three days he was sent to the infirmary. This had five rooms, of which the greatest was, in the time of Hugh, twenty-seven feet wide and thirty-three feet long,[3] and its own cloister. There the Prior or his deputy visited the ailing monk, and if necessary ordered him meat. If he were well enough he went to the first Mass and to the beginning of the second, leaning on a staff, wearing his night boots, and with his cowl over his eyes; and sang Sext in the chapel of St.

---

[1] Migne, 753.   [2] Herrgot, 186; Albers, *Cons. Farf.*, 186.
[3] Albers, *Cons. Farf.*, 137. It had eight beds and eight latrines in an adjoining building. It was rebuilt later and enlarged to 76 feet long by 33 feet wide (L'Huillier, *Vie de Saint Hugues*, 629).

Mary.[1] When he came into the infirmary refectory[2] he found his chair set ready and his little table laid with his bread and wine and platter. The keeper of the infirmary brought in his food, and the infirmary servants waited on him; if he needed anything he struck the table with his knife to summon one.

After dinner he rested, or meditated in the infirmary chapel, and went to bed immediately after supper. When he was well again, he asked for his day shoes; and at Prime or Tierce stood at the door of the chapel of St. Mary until the children passed, when he joined them and went into church. At the following Chapter he rose, and asked pardon: 'Mea culpa, in Infirmaria fui, nostrum ordinem sicut debuissem non custodivi'; to which the Abbot replied, 'Noster Dominus te absolvat de omnibus in quibus offendisti.' The brother then bowed to the Abbot and the other brothers, who returned his greeting; the Abbot ordered him to recite seven paternosters or the seven penitential psalms, and he took up ordinary life once more.

If, however, the monk's condition did not improve, but worsened, he kept his bed altogether, and the keeper of the infirmary told the Prior, who ordered the cellarer to send one or more of his servants to nurse and tend him.[3] If the invalid felt he was in danger of death he confessed to the Abbot or Prior and asked for the last Sacraments.[4] Two brothers carried him into the Chapter, where he charged himself with all his sins against God and the brethren, and the Abbot absolved him. They bore him back to the infirmary, and laid him on a low bed. After the Chapter, the priest in alb and stole came bearing the holy oil, accompanied by lay brethren with holy water, crucifix, and candles, and followed by the community singing the *Miserere*. While the community sang, the priest, with thumb dipped in the oil traced the Cross on his eyes, his ears, his lips, his nose, his hands, his feet, and his body, saying: 'Per istam

---

[1] During Lent, if he were well enough, he sang Nones and Vespers immediately afterwards.

[2] There was one part for those who ate meat, and one for those who did not.

[3] Under Raingarde and her granddaughters Marguerite and Poncie de Montboissier, the nunnery at Marcigny became a centre of medical and nursing skill. See Pet. Ven., *Epist.*, vi. 39.   [4] Herrgot, 190; Albers, *Cons. Farf.*, 192.

unctionem, et suam piissimam misericordiam indulgeat tibi Dominus quidquid peccasti per visum, per auditum, per gustum, per odoratum, per tactum, per incessum, per ardorem libidinis.'

The priest fetched the Reserved Elements from the church and gave the sick man communion: then the dying monk kissed the crucifix,[1] and in farewell gave the kiss of peace to the priest, the brethren, and the oblates. The community returned chanting to the church, leaving one of the brothers to watch and pray by his friend's bed-side. When death seemed near, the infirmary servants laid a hair shirt on the floor, sprinkled it with ashes, and laid the dying man upon it. One knocked a double knock on the cloister door to summon the brethren, who hastened to the bed-side. There, if he yet lived, they repeated the Athanasian Creed and the litanies of the Saints and for the dying. When death had come, the priest prayed for his soul, and the community went to the chapel of St. Mary to sing the Vespers of the Dead. The lay brethren tolled all the bells; the priest censed and asperged the body; and it was prepared for burial. The body was dressed in the Regular robe, cape, and night shoes; the cowl was lowered over the face and sewn down upon the robe; the cape was wrapped round and sewn together, and over all was passed a shroud made of black serge like the robe. The body was once more censed and asperged, and laid in an open coffin. The brethren were summoned, and accompanied the coffin, praying as they went, to the chapel of St. Mary. After more prayers it was brought into the great church to the tolling of the bells, and set there with a crucifix and candles at its head. That day or the next the funeral took place after the morning Mass or after Vespers. One of the great bells was struck three times, and all assembled in the church and received lighted candles from the sacristan. After the usual prayers all went in procession by the chapel of St. Mary (where such invalids as were well enough awaited them) to the cemetery, where they ranged themselves round the grave. The coffin was covered and the lid

---

[1] In his revised statutes of 1132 Peter the Venerable prescribes that this shall not be a crucifix of gold or silver, but one of wood with a painted figure, enclosing a relic of the true cross. He ordered all the houses of the Order to procure a cross similar to that used at Cluny.

nailed down; and the body of the dead brother was laid to rest. That day every monk who was a priest said Mass for his soul; the next day, what food was left from dinner was given to the poor on his behalf. For seven days the Office and Mass were sung for him; psalm or prayer was recited for him after each Regular hour; for thirty days a private Mass was celebrated for him, and his allowance of food was given to the poor; and news of his death and a request for prayers for the peace of his soul was sent to every Cluniac house in Christendom.

VI
ART AND LETTERS AT CLUNY

THE reading of books was a part of the daily life of the monastery, and brought into its tradition an element of literary culture. According to the Benedictine Rule the monks read in the cloister from the fourth to the sixth hour between Easter and October, and after Sext might either read in the cloister or rest on their beds. In the short winter days there was only time for an hour's reading; but with Lent the time was again increased. On Sundays reading was permitted at any time between the offices and meals.

At Cluny, besides private reading, there was much reading aloud both in church, refectory, and chapter-house. At Septuagesima, Genesis was begun for the night office, and finished in a week; Exodus followed at Sexagesima, and it and the succeeding books of the Bible were read in both church and refectory, so that the first eight books of the Old Testament were finished by Ash Wednesday. Augustine on the Psalms was read at Nocturns during Lent; the Prophecies of Jeremiah in the first days of Holy Week; part of the Acts of the Apostles during the octave of Easter; Revelation and the Epistles in the fortnight following. The Acts were continued from Ascension to Whitsun, but as the nights were getting shorter less was read at Nocturns and more in the refectory. The books of Kings, the Song of Solomon, the books of Job, Tobit, Judith, Esther, Esdras, and Maccabees were read during the summer. In November with lengthening nights more was read at Nocturns. Ezekiel lasted until Martinmas; Daniel, the twelve minor prophets, and Gregory's commentary on Ezekiel were read between then and Advent. During Advent, Isaiah was read, together with the epistles of Pope Leo on the Incarnation, and the Commentary of Augustine. After Christmas came the Epistles of St. Paul, with Chrysostom's treatise on the Epistle to the Hebrews if there was time for it.[1] At the Chapter part of the Benedictine Rule was read and commented on every morning, and

---

[1] Migne, 643 and 659.

every evening there was more reading, generally from the *Collationes* of the Fathers, the study of which St. Benedict had recommended to all those who would seek perfection.

The library at Cluny was kept in a closet called the *Armarium*, opening off the cloister.[1] A list of some of the books in the time of Odilo[2] includes a remarkable number of books on the Lives and Passions of the Saints. A later and fuller catalogue[3] shows the library to have been unusually rich. Naturally it contained the books needed for the daily life of church and cloister: Old and New Testaments, homilies, sermons, and lives of saints, the works of Gregory, Augustine, and Chrysostom. Its collection of the Fathers was fairly complete: Orosius, Basil, Tertullian, Eusebius, Ambrose, Jerome, Priscian, Isidore, Cassian, Origen, Caesarius, Hilary, Cassiodorus, and their successors the pseudo-Dionysius, Hrabanus Maurus, Walafrid Strabo, Bede, Alcuin, Anselm of Bec, and Lanfranc. It contained copies of all the chief coenobitic and eremitic Rules of early times: Basil, Pachomius, Fructuosus, Faustus, Isidore, and Columban, and Smaragdus' *Diadema Monachorum*, and of the usual grammatical works, Priscian, Donatus, Macrobius, Servius, and Martianus Capella.

Civil and Canon Law were represented by a book of Papal decrees, another of decrees of Church Councils, the Decretals, Theodosius' manual of Roman Law, the Institutes of Gaius, and a copy of the Salic Law. Other books of practical use were Boethius on Arithmetic, Guy of Arezzo on Music, and a treatise on medicaments. The historical section was rich and varied. It naturally included writings concerning Cluny—the works of Odo, Maiol, Odilo and Peter the Venerable, and their lives; the letters of Peter Damian, Fulbert, Bernard of Clairvaux and others—but its scope was much wider than this. It included a history of the Franks, the chronicle of Ado, Archbishop of Vienne, a history of the Vandal and Lombard Church, the *Historia tripartita*, the *Vita*

---

[1] Pignot, ii. 419.

[2] Albers, *Cons. Farf.*, 185; and see Wilmart in Cabrol and Leclercq, *Dictionnaire d'archéologie chrétienne*, iii, pt. 2, col. 2074, s.v. Cluny, manuscrits liturgiques de.

[3] Delisle, *Catalogue des fonds de Cluny*, Appendix I, p. 337, dates it to the middle of the twelfth century, but I do not think it can be earlier than 1200. When Mabillon visited Cluny at the beginning of the eighteenth century he was shown a catalogue made five hundred years before with nearly 1,800 entries.

Karoli, the Chronicle of Bishop Friculf, the *Origo et gesta francorum* up to the time of William of Aquitaine, and a history of the Lombards in seven books; and a fairly representative collection of classical historians: Livy, Suetonius, Sallust, Josephus, Pompeius Trogus, and a book on the lives and deaths of the Emperors from Augustus to Theodosius. Science was represented by Pliny, Solinus, Vitruvius on Architecture, Serenus on medicine, and the *Physiognomon*.[1] A surprising number of the works of the orators and poets of antiquity was to be found on its shelves: the *Bucolics*, *Georgics*, and *Aeneid*, with the commentary of Servius; a remarkably complete collection of the works of Cicero[2]; two copies of Horace; Juvenal; three copies of Terence; Ovid, *de arte amatoria* and *de remedio amoris*; Statius; Lucan; Claudianus; Apuleius; the Fables of Avianus; the *Somnium Scipionis*; a life of Alexander of Macedon; the romance of Apollonius of Tyre, and *libri mythologiarum*. Philosophy was represented by Chalcidius' translation of the *Timaeus*, with its commentary, by the *Ten Categories* of Aristotle, by Boethius on the *Consolations of philosophy*,[3] and by a treatise of Philo the Jew.

The Rule of St. Benedict prescribed that each monk should read one book during Lent,[4] and at Cluny books were issued to the brethren at that season by the precentor, who had charge of the library. Every year on the second day of Lent a brother demanded the return of those already issued, and, list in hand, checked those which each monk laid on the table before him. If the book returned had not for any reason been read, pardon had to be asked. The list of books

[1] Physiologus?
[2] A ninth-century MS. of his Orations from Cluny is now at Holkham: a page is reproduced in E. Châtelain, *Paléographie des classiques latins*, Plate 27.
[3] Books which it is difficult to identify are 'Dindimus de gente brachmanorum' and 'Historia Egesippi'. The surviving early Catalogues of Moissac (Delisle, *Cabinet des Manuscrits*, ii. 441) are not complete: they enumerate service-books and patristic works. That of Maillezais (ibid., ii. 506) is also probably incomplete: the books enumerated are mostly devotional and patristic, with a copy of the *Gesta Anglorum* but no classical texts. Those of Limoges (ibid., i. 395, ii. 493; Duplès-Agier, p. 323) include a considerable number of such texts, but not as many as the catalogue of Cluny. A few books were kept even in the granges, but sometimes these seem to have been neglected; a letter from Abbot Peter to Guigo, Prior of the Chartreuse, asks for the loan of a volume of the letters of St. Augustine: 'for the greater part of our copy, that was in one of our granges, has been accidentally eaten by a bear' (*Epist*. i. 24; Marrier, 653).
[4] *Regula*, cap. xlviii; Woelflin, 49.

given out in Lent in 1042 or 1043 has survived,[1] and includes, besides theological and devotional works, several books of history—Eusebius, Orosius, Bede, Josephus, and Livy. A later list, that for 1252,[2] includes a herbal, a book of prognostications, a history of the kings of Britain and Jerusalem, a book 'de pictura rote',[3] a book on animals, a work in Hebrew, and a book in verse, not otherwise specified. The register of borrowers ends with a list of eleven missing books. Books were lent not only within the monastery but also to other houses of the Order; the list of 1252 shows no less than 128 works to have been so lent.[4] Books were borrowed and lent even outside the Order, but Abbot Hugh made a rule that no book should be so lent except on receipt of an adequate surety.[5]

Naturally such reading as was carried on at Cluny encouraged theological studies. Peter the Venerable has left us a portrait of the monkish theologian in his description of Brother Gregory. He was the one truly happy man that Peter knew; for all his life was passed in theological speculation, and all his being found satisfaction in it. He went round the Cluniac houses working in their libraries, collating texts, discovering difficult questions in order that he might have the pleasure of answering them.

'Wherever the business of the Order calls me', wrote Peter, 'in all our houses and even in their darkest corners, I find Gregory with his Sermons, Gregory with his Epistles, Gregory with treatises, with a pile of books and notes. I see you everywhere, and everywhere in the same surroundings; the lap of your robe is full of books, your knees give way beneath their weight.'

But the library at Cluny gave encouragement not only to theological studies. Many of the brethren were not altogether unversed in profane literature, and could profit by the study of the classics. When Abbot Odo was a canon of Tours he studied Virgil, until he had a dream of a vase

---

[1] In the *Consuetudines Farfenses*, ed. Albers, p. 185. For a study of it see Wilmart in *Revue Mabillon*, xi, 1921, 89.
[2] Delisle, *Cabinet des Manuscrits*, ii. 481.   [3] On the Wheel of Fortune?
[4] Delisle, *Inventaire des MSS. de la Bibliothèque Nationale; fonds de Cluni*, lx and Appendix II, 373.
[5] See Pet. Ven., *Epist.*, i. 24; Marrier, 651.

beautiful in form but filled with serpents, which he inter-
preted as a symbol of the pernicious doctrines which Virgil
poetically expressed; and so renounced him for the study of
the Gospels and Prophets.[1] Maiol, again, studied the classics
at Lyons before he came to Cluny; and we are told that when
he was appointed Librarian, 'having himself read the philo-
sophers of old and the lies of Virgil, he no longer desired
either to read them himself or to let others do so'. Hugh also
studied Virgil until his scruples were aroused. One night,
as he fell asleep, he seemed to see a heap of serpents lying
under his head. He woke in horror and could not sleep,
until he found a volume of Virgil under his pillow. Casting
it out, he fell asleep, and awoke convinced of the poisonous
nature of poetic fictions.[2]

Such stories in themselves show the charm that the
classics had for Cluniac minds, and it is not surprising that
the Cistercians upbraided the Cluniacs for their classical
learning. In the 'Dialogue between a Cluniac and a Cistercian'[3] the Cistercian says: 'By your speech, by your quotations from the poets, I recognize a Cluniac, for you and your
brethren take so much pleasure in the lies of poets, that you
read, study, and teach them even in the hours which St.
Benedict has definitely reserved for the reading of the Scriptures and manual labour.' The Cluniac justifies the practice
as a means to an end: 'If we read the books of the pagans, it
is to make ourselves perfect in their language, and thus to fit
us better to understand the Scriptures; for in our Order, as
you know, the reading of sacred books and prayer succeed
each other without intermission. From reading we pass to
prayer, and from prayer we return to reading.'

Certainly the earliest literary work written at Cluny was
all devotional or theological in character. It arose, indeed,
naturally out of the needs of the monastery. Odo, himself
dedicated to St. Martin from childhood, wished hymns in his
honour to be sung on his festival, and had to provide them

---

[1] Marrier, 422.

[2] The writings of Odo show his acquaintance with the works of Virgil, Priscian,
and Martianus Capella, and betray some slight knowledge of Greek (Sandys,
A History of Classical Scholarship, i. 505).

[3] Martène, *Thesaurus nov. anecdot.*, v. 1573. Peter the Venerable writes to Peter
of Poitiers against the sole study of the classics (Marrier, 631; *Epist.*, i. 9) but was
himself a good scholar.

himself[1]; he wished his monks to study the *Moralia* of Gregory, and had to abbreviate them for their use; and he similarly supplemented the *Collationes* of the Fathers with *Collationes* of his own, in which he shows himself a minor prophet of tenth-century France. His sermons in verse and prose and his life of Gerald of Aurillac were equally connected with his official life; his most personal works were a poem on the Eucharist,[2] a hymn in honour of the Magdalen, and his most famous poem, the *Occupatio*.[3]

The hymn in honour of the Magdalen is a typical piece of medieval rhymed verse admirably adapted to chanting:[4]

> Lauda mater Ecclesia,
> lauda Christi clementiam:
> qui septem purgat vitia
> per septiformem gratiam.
> Maria soror Lazari
> quae tot commisit crimina,
> ab ipsa fauce tartari
> redit ad vitae praemia.
> Post fluxae carnis scandala
> fit ex lebete phiala;
> in vas translata gloriae
> de vase contumeliae.
> Aegra currit ad Medicum
> vas ferens aromaticum:
> et a morbo multiplici
> verbo curatur Medici.

[1] See Raby, 311. The fourth is a curious metrical piece that attempts an internal rhyme in each line:

> tu pacem reparas hic et ad astra migras
> nunc nos te medio concilies domino
> Odonis famuli, hoc opus qui condidi
> Emigrando de saeculo.

[2] Marrier, 263.

> Convivas epuli mundos Deus esse superni
> ut docet, et servis Dominus vestigia lavit.
> Muneribus variis, et pluribus inde reiectis,
> frumentum et vinum cunctis hoc protulit unum.
> Hoc sacrat, hoc nimium, quod fit breue, quod nimis altum,
> tam modicum sumptum, tam facile atque paratum;
> tam sublime tamen quod totam habeat deitatem,
> sufficit hoc solum mundi purgare piaclum.
> Hinc placet hoc munus, quod fit de pluribus unum
> Corpus hinc capiti, caput inde cohaeret in illi;
> hoc genus, hoc unum placet, hoc durabit in aevum,
> hoc facile est, nitidum, simplex, deitateque plenum.

[3] Ed. Swoboda, in the Teubner Texts. See Raby, 312.   [4] Marrier, 263.

Contriti cordis punctio
cum lachrymarum fluvio,
et pietatis actio,
ream solvit a vitio.
Surgentem cum victoria
Jesum videt ab inferis;
prima meretur gaudia
quae plus ardebat caeteris.
Uni Deo sit gloria
pro multiplici gratia:
qui culpas, et flagitia
remittit, et dat praemia.

The *Occupatio* is even more typically monastic in its obscure and difficult language, its theological subject, its gloomy moralizing, and its recondite allegory. The themes of its seven books are the creation of the world, the fall of the angels, the making of man and the origin of sin, the growth of wickedness, the plan of redemption, and the foundation of the Church. There are reminiscences of Horace and Juvenal, Sedulius and Prudentius, but for the most part these are reminiscences of vituperation.[1] Occasionally some whisper of calm or beauty is echoed from Odo's earlier Virgilian studies:

Aere jam sudo tellus hiemale fugato
frigore, sol placidas cum dat vicinior auras,
vere novo faciem praetendit ubique venustam,
quolibet ad varios laxat cum viscera foetus,
germina cum laeti produnt sibi credita sulci,
picturant varii cum prata virentia flores,
frondibus arboreis folio fructuve repletis
garrula vox avium cum per convallia tinnit,
hinnulus enixae cum se sugit ubera cervae,
mater ovis proprium noscit balatibus agnum.

but such whispers are few and faint.

When Odo died his disciple John of Salerno wrote his life,

[1] Odo's use of Greek words is perhaps also worthy of notice; e.g. l. 16 et seqq.:
Hoc topon atque usian, telon dat rebus et archin,
non minor in minimis maiorve probatur in amplis,
ast tamen ut micros megalos quoque vel quasi sues,
dum minima affectu magna et medioxima dulci
intimus obgirat refovensque forinsecus implet.
A similar knowledge of Virgil and Horace is also shown in the *Visio* of Ansellus Scholasticus, a monk of Saint-Benoît, written at Odo's request (Raby, 257; Du Méril, p. 200).

and founded thereby a Cluniac tradition of sound and interesting narrative. Even to-day the *Vita Odonis*, with its skilful characterization, its lively dialogue, and its power of creating a picture in the mind, makes good reading. The biographical tradition was carried on by Abbot Odilo, who wrote a short life of Maiol to be read on his anniversary—notable for its more flowing and literary style—and a life of the Empress Adelaide, besides a set of sermons of a traditional type for the great feasts. Even his verse-writings are on similar themes—a short dirge for Adelaide, and hymns for the vigil of Maiol's anniversary, and for Nocturns, Lauds, and Vespers on that day. These hymns curiously illustrate the double type of Latin verse in his day. The hymn for Lauds [1] is in rhymed verse:

> Maiole consors procerum
> Regum Regi placentium;
> inter coelestes aulicos
> divinitatis conscios.
>
> Honoris privilegio
> coetu junctus monastico:
> sed et choris angelicis
> frueris aula luminis.
>
> Unde Pater nos respice
> pressos peccati pondere:
> depone gravem sarcinam,
> laeviga conscientiam.
>
> Hic fascibus depositis
> mortis solutos vinculis:
> junge nos tuos servulos
> monachis praestantissimis.
>
> Cum quibus nos perpetua
> possideamus gaudia:
> Christi favente gratia
> per infinita secula.   Amen.

[1] Marrier, 292. Cf. his hymn on the Assumption of the Virgin (Marrier, 406), which begins:

> Adest dies laetitiae
> jocundus omni lumine
> in quo Regina Virginum
> scandit iter astriferum.
> Angelorum praefulgidis
> circumvallata cuneis:
> quamque sanctarum Virginum
> sequitur agmen inclitum.

Another hymn of the Maiol cycle is reprinted in *Revue Bénédictine*, xxxviii, 1926, p. 53.

Whereas that for the second Vespers is in Sapphics curiously modified by inner rhymes: [1]

> Christe cunctorum pariter tuorum
> palmitum vitis, Deus alme nobis
> praebe Maioli celebrare tanti
> festa patroni.
>
> Quem tibi nostris placuit diebus,
> pluribus signis meritisque dignis,
> regibus coram hominumque turmis
> glorificare.
>
> Annuas istisque sic interesse
> gaudiis nos perpetuis et amplis
> pro reis gestis merito carere
> ut nequeamus.
>
> Quaesumus rector pietatis auctor,
> noster hic pastor tibi sit precator,
> quo tua nobis pietate cunctis
> crimina dones.
>
> Cujus in tanto pia vota festo
> congruit nobis iugiter canendo,
> insuper paschae tibi duplicatas
> solvere laudes.
>
> Trinitas Deus unus atque summus,
> sit tibi Rex gloria sempiterna,
> qui regis tanta bonitate cuncta
> omne per aevum.
> Amen.

In the time of Odilo one of the best-known Cluniac writers came to the abbey: Radulphus Glaber, Ralph the Bald, who after wandering from one Benedictine abbey to another came to end his days at Cluny. There, about 1047, he wrote his 'Five books of Histories', and dedicated them to Odilo. He writes his prologue as one resuscitating the writing of history after a lapse of some two hundred years; and indeed he brings to history something of the same natural liveliness that John of Salerno brought to biography. He is at his best when describing something—such as the plague at Cluny [2]—that he has known at first hand.

---

[1] Marrier, 292.   [2] p. 23.

In the work of Jotsaldus, a monk of Cluny who wrote a *Planctus* or dirge for Odilo, a new dramatic quality is evident in form and style. The whole is written as a miniature drama in dialogue.[1] It begins:

Ad fletus voces extendat chorda sonoras,
organa cunctorum vertantur sorte modorum.
Plangite vos populi, vos linguae sydera coeli,
proruat in tenebras resplendens orbita Solis,
deficiant plene radiantia cornua Lunae,
lugeat et mundus protenso corpore totus:
nunc terras, pelagus, montes, silvasque ciebo:
quadrupedes, bipedes, reptantia cuncta movebo.
Condoleant Patrem subtractum nunc Odilonem,
conciso plausu, pungantur viscera fletu,
et variis lachrymas profundant vocibus istas,
Odilo dulce decus venturi gloria secli,
Odilo dulce decus, fraternae pacis amicus,
Odilo dulce decus meritorum lampade clarus . . .

Reason replies, that 'quod nequit absolvi, debet patienter haberi', and this is followed by a 'Revelatio doloris, et consolatio mortis', with the same triple use of name:

Musa mihi causas memora, quo tristia solvam
deponens lacrymas steriles, et gaudia sumam.
Odilo non moritur, sed mortis funera spernit:
Odilo non moritur, sed vitam duxit honestam:
Odilo non moritur, sed vitam morte recepit.
Regnat in aeternum gaudens se cernere Christum
quem coluit, docuit, quaesivit, glorificavit,
cuius gloria crux fuit, et Christus crucifixus. . .

It ends with an Epilogue addressed to Odilo, partly inspired by the Song of Songs:

Odilo dilectus, nunc candidus et rubicundus,
securo incessu sequitur vestigia Christi,
floridus et niveus, defertur lectulus illi
quem tegit alta cedrus, redolensque cupressus adornat:
sparguntur violae, sternuntur lilia quaeque . . .

[1] Marrier, 329. I have come across no evidence for religious drama at Cluny itself, but the earliest-known instances of an Easter trope of dramatic form and of a Latin ritual drama of the Magi are from the Cluniac monastery of Saint-Martial-de-Limoges (Raby, 220; Anz, *Die Lateinischen Magier-Spiele*, Leipzig, 1925). A drama of the wise and foolish virgins was also played there at an early date (Mâle, *Art religieux en France au XIIe siècle*, 148).

Under Hugh, literature seems to have languished at Cluny; the planning and building of the great basilica was the chief artistic creation of his time. His epitaph,[1] however, is graceful, if a less curious literary exercise than the *Planctus* of Jotsaldus:

> Regula Virtutum, pater Hugo decus Monachorum
> spes inopum, contemptor opum, portus miserorum,
> vas templumque Dei, libamen et hostia Christi,
> carne locatur humi, sed spiritus astra petivit.
> O felix currus! felix auriga tuorum!
> Fac ut ad astras vehas, quos hic vivendo regebas.
> Ultima lux vitae, penultima luxit Aprilis,
> lux aeterna Deus, tibi luceat omne per aevum.

When Pons de Melgueil succeeded him, he had to have the literary work he ordered written outside the abbey: the life of Hugh by Hildebert of Le Mans,[2] and a commentary on Proverbs by Richard of Fourneaux.

Under Peter the Venerable, however, there was a great revival of literature at Cluny. Clear logical treatises on Justice and Mercy, the Eucharist, and Free Will were produced by Alger of Liége,[3] who also compiled a collection of deeds and charters concerning the abbey; Peter of Pithiviers wrote a treatise on the monastic life, 'proses' to the Virgin, and other religious verse; Richard of Poitiers wrote a rather dry general chronicle from the Fall of Adam to 1155; and Peter of Poitiers a good deal of imitative verse, including a *Panegyric* of Peter the Venerable.

The Abbot himself wrote[4] to Brother Gislebert—whose letter to him he had had, for want of leisure, to read during the Epistle—'If indeed it is true, as Scripture says, that "the wisdom of a learned man cometh by opportunity of leisure, and he that hath little business shall become wise",[5] then how shall I ever attain to writing anything near wisdom, who have no leisure, whose whole life is one endless and most tiresome business?' None the less, Peter produced a con-

---

[1] *Hist. lit. de la France*, ix. 474.
[2] Based on a very simply written life by Hugh's disciples Gilon and Etzelon, published by L'Huillier, p. 574.
[3] d. 1131; Marrier, 594.
[4] *Epist.*, i. 20; Marrier 6 o   [5] Ecclesiasticus xxxviii. 24.

siderable and varied literary output. Besides the necessary
sermons, of which four survive, he wrote three theological
treatises in which scriptural quotations and analogies are combined with strict logical method: one against the Petrobrusians
and Henricians, one against the Jews, attempting to refute
their errors out of the Old Testament, and a third against
the Mohammedans.[1] He carried on the historiographical
tradition of Cluny in his treatise *de Miraculis*, which recounts
with considerable narrative power and some lively dialogue
the lives of the great men of the Order, and the miracles performed in his time and in that of his predecessor in all the
Cluniac houses. The most accomplished and the most personal of his prose writings are the *Letters*, finished, graceful,
almost artificial in style, that already prelude Petrarch's,
though set in another key. It is the phrases and diction of
the Psalms that most often recur in them; but there is many
a phrase modelled on Horace, Virgil, and Cicero, classical
allusions are not wanting, and there is often a classical grace
in the turn of the phrase and the aptness of the thought.
A typical example of his style is the letter he wrote to the
nuns of Marcigny after the death of his mother Raingarde,
who had taken the veil in their convent.[2] After describing
her last moments, and thanking the nuns for receiving her,
he continues:

'Now this humble handmaid of God and yourselves lies buried
under your pious eyes, and although lifeless and silent, yet
addresses to you, if you give ear, earnest and frequent prayers.
She is always appearing before your eyes, that you may remember
her and that you may not forget yourselves. A sister, she speaks
to her sisters; and dead, she addresses the living. She shows you
what she is now and what you soon shall be. She recalls to you
the place where you shall be buried, the sphere to which your soul
shall take its flight. You have ever before your eyes the graves,
the homes of our mortal natures, in which you hope to find rest for
so long as death shall keep his dominion, and whence you hope to
rise when death shall be vanquished. May this sight be a never-
ending lesson to you; may the vanishing of temporal things,

[1] When travelling in Spain he had the Koran translated at Toledo in order that
he might endeavour to refute it. Pignot, iii. 536. One of the translators was an
Englishman, Robert Kennet; the translation was afterwards verified by an Arab.
[2] *Epist.*, ii. 17.

which you witness every day, inspire you to desire yet more
ardently the things that are eternal. Even as a man sows the seeds
of trees in a garden, so do they bury your bodies in the holy ground
of the graveyard, that, as the apostle says, cannot be quickened
except they die. You must needs bear with courage the winter of
your present life, the chill of snow and rain, while the beauty and
fruitfulness of the trees yet sleep, while it is not yet manifest what
you will one day be, while your life is yet hid with Christ in God.
But a time shall come when the air shall recover its calm and an
endless spring shall follow the icy blasts; a sun that shall never set
shall arise, and shall drive the shadows away before its shining
beams and shall bring heat instead of cold, and, flooding the world
with a light such as the earth has never known, shall vanquish
ancient night before nature's astonished gaze, and bring a day that
shall know no ending. In this time of marvels the fruitful earth
shall bring forth new flowers and new fruit from the seed of your
bodies. That which was corruptible shall put on incorruptibility;
that which was mortal, immortality.'

Peter the Venerable was also an accomplished verse-
writer. He wrote an apology for Pierre de Poitiers *Panegyric*, and several epitaphs, of which the best-known is that
on Abelard.[1] Peter also carried on the Cluniac tradition
of sacred verse-writing. Like Odo, he wrote a hymn in
honour of the Magdalen, and another in honour of Hugh
of Cluny.[2] Since—he declared—the hymn used for the
festival of St. Benedict contained at least twenty-four mis-
takes and no moral teaching, he wrote a new one; and also
wrote a hymn, shorter than that hitherto in use, for the
celebration of the translation of the Saint's body to Fleury.
His verses on the Resurrection and in honour of the Saviour
show a research of elaboration in their prosody that is

[1] Marrier, 1354.

> Gallorum Socrates, Plato maximus Hesperiarum,
> noster Aristoteles, Logicis quicunque fuerunt,
> aut par, aut melior: studiorum cognitus orbi
> princeps, ingenio varius, subtilis et acer:
> omnia vi superans rationis, et arte loquendi,
> Abelardus erat. Sed tunc magis omnia vicit,
> cum Cluniacensem monachum, moremque professus,
> ad Christi veram transivit Philosophiam,
> in qua longaevae bene complens ultima vitae,
> philosophis quandoque bonis se connumerandum
> spem dedit, undenas Maio renovante calendas.

[2] Ibid., 466.

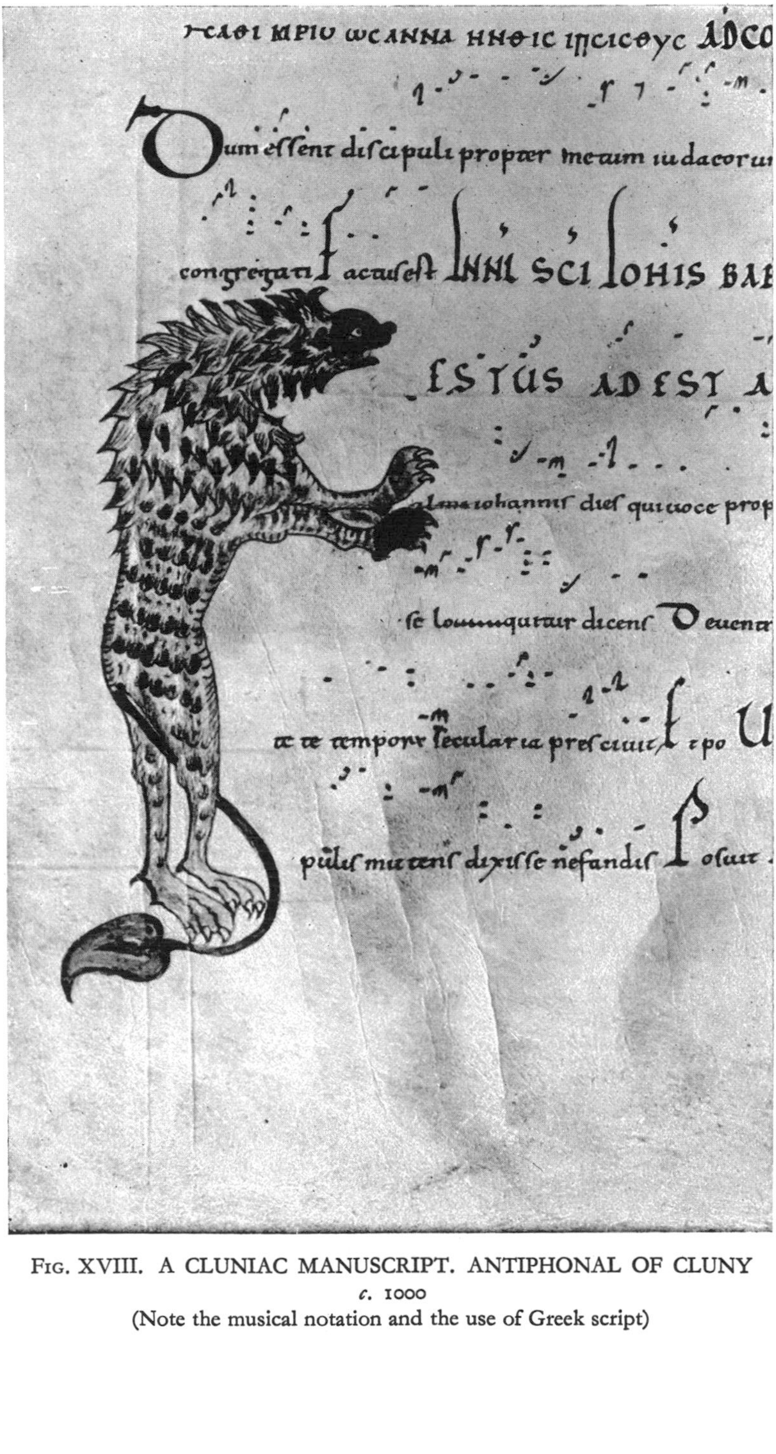

Fig. XVIII. A CLUNIAC MANUSCRIPT. ANTIPHONAL OF CLUNY
c. 1000
(Note the musical notation and the use of Greek script)

characteristic of his day. The first is a curious literary exercise beginning:

Mortis portis fortis vim intulit,
Crucem ducem illius perculit,[1]

while the second [2] goes with a swing in spite of its complicated rhymes:

A Patre mittitur, in terris nascitur, Deus de Virgine.
Humana patitur, docet et moritur libens pro homine.
Per lignum vetitum sumpsit interitum nostra mortalitas.
Ligni patibulo redditur seculo amissa dignitas.
Fructus comeditur, quo vita perditur, de mortis arbore.
Sanguis effunditur, qui fide sumitur, de Christi corpore . . .

It reaches real fervour with its description of the Last Day and Judgement; and then Peter remembers that he and his flock will share in that awful resurrection.

Christe, deus meus, ad te clamo reus, quem spero judicem :
ut tunc clementiam, non iram sentiam malorum vindicem . . .
Cluniacensium sis memor ovium in tanto turbine
et ad perpetua duc ea pascua benigne domine.

Most of his sacred poems were written not at Cluny itself, but when for rest and recreation he joined one of the colonies of hermit-monks on the neighbouring hills. In 1147 he wrote to Peter of Pithiviers: 'Wearied with dwelling in towns, we live in the forests and love the meadows:

"Jam non mihi turbida regia Romae
Sed vacuum Tibur placet, ac imbelle Tarentum."

Veterans old enough to retire, we leave war to younger men, to you and those of your age. Take up your arms, march to battle, pit yourselves against the enemy. Since the whole world goes to arms,[3] join the host of the men of war. . . . Yet I would not have my retirement, that you charge with idleness, be completely idle. To avail myself once more of the words of the poet:

"Me doctarum hederae praemia frontium
Diis miscent superis; me gelidum nemus"

but I will not add "secernunt populo".'[4]

---

[1] Marrier, 1348.
[3] i.e. to Crusade.
[2] Marrier, 1344; Raby, 313.
[4] *Epist.*, iv. 30.

In such circumstances the familiar atmosphere of the cloister was forgotten under the open sky. In the clearings of the forest religion itself became more beautiful. 'When you come', writes Brother Robert, 'you will find neither hermitage nor hermits; we have a Parnassus with a triple peak, and not a double like that of which the ancient poets speak; do not seek here hornéd fauns or dancing satyrs, but cowled poets, monks robed in black, brethren devoted to piety, prayer, and reading.'

It was there that Abbot Peter wrote the most finished of his poems, a letter to Raymond, a monk of Toulouse, who had written asking that he might accompany him to Rome. It begins with a classical compliment:

Cum caput albescat, tua Musa senescere nescit:
    nec quia tu canes, hinc minus illa canit.
Albus es, et cantas: albos imitaris olores
    quorum juncta magis, voxque nitorque placent.
Hinc color obtusus, sonus hinc demulcet et aures.
    Sic nihil in tota non placet amnis ave.
Non norat volucres nutrire Garonna canoras,
    littora nunc cuius cantibus implet olor.
Fleverat antiquis viduata Tholosa Poëtis:
    gaudeat en studium te reparare suum.
Scribis Romanas te cernere velle ruinas.
    Si tentare mihi, tale placeret iter.
Dum lego forte tui mirandos pectoris ausus,
    obstupui fateor, conticuique diu . . .
Non eris ingratus, quem novit reddere charum
    fama frequens, studium, vita, senile caput.
Ornabis totam nota probitate cohortem,
    virtutumque viris signifer unus eris.
Pulchrior in sylvis nusquam frondescit oliva,
    dum candore suo deprimit omne virens . . .' [1]

Perhaps it was there, too, that Peter studied and criticized the text of the greatest of Cluniac poems [2]: the *De contemptu mundi* dedicated to him by the Cluniac monk, Bernard of Morval or Morlaas. [3] This is the most finished example of

[1] *Epist.*, iv. 23; Marrier, 855.
[2] Bernard in his Preface alludes to Peter's critical help, and develops a theory of the balance between form and content in verse (*De contemptu mundi*, ed. Hoskier, 1929, p. xxxv).
[3] On his identity see J. W. Thompson in *Journal of Theological Studies*, 1906–7, viii. 394, and Hoskier in his Preface to his edition of the poem.

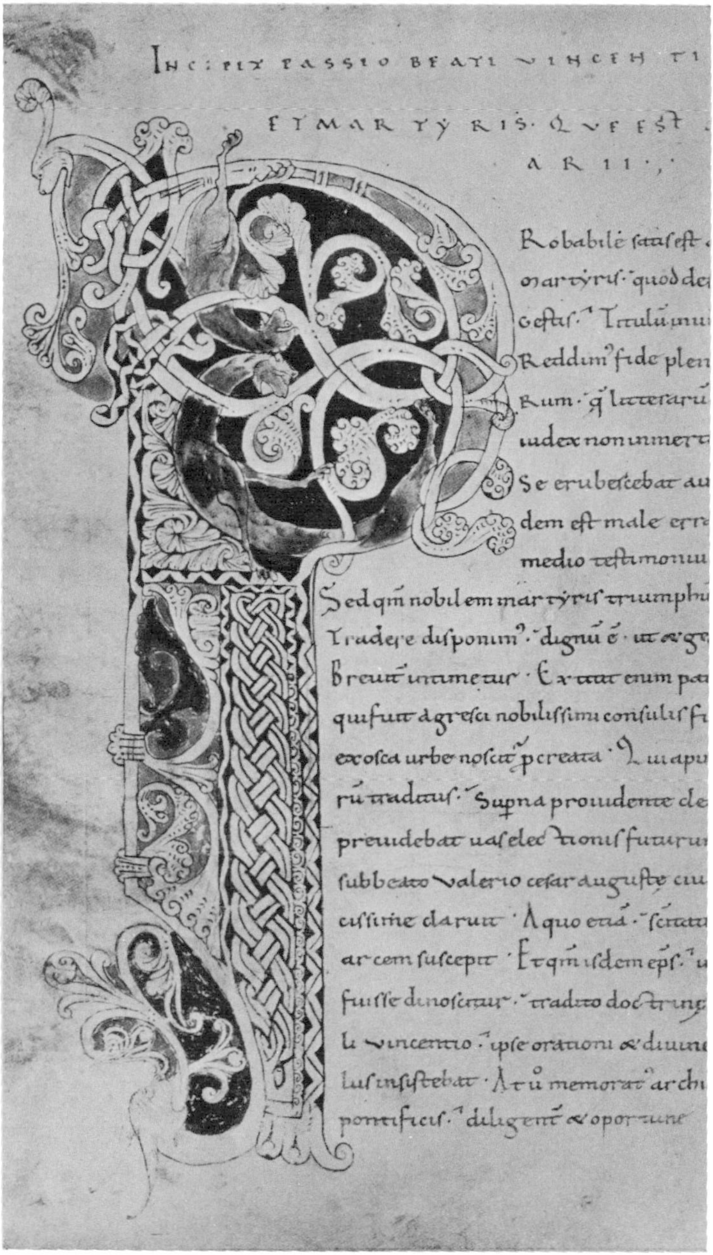

Fig. XIX. A CLUNIAC INITIAL. LIVES OF SAINTS
End of eleventh century

Cluniac prosody in its rhythmic devices, its assonances and
alliterations, its repetitions and antitheses, its classical
allusions [1] and its verbal virtuosities; yet it transcends mere
metrical skill. Bernard's poem remains memorable both for
the sounding onrush of his verse and also for the force and
vigour of his indictment of this world and the beatitude of
his vision of the world to come. Both are felt and real:
through his verses, that in translation are familiar to every
English-speaking Protestant,[2] sound echoes of the troubles
that had rent the congregation of Cluny and of the Cluniac
vision of Christian unity that yet survived.

Nil ibi debile, nil ibi flebile, nil ibi scissum;
res ibi publica, pax erit unica, pax in id ipsum.
Hic furor, hic mala scismata, scandala, pax sine pace;
pax sine litibus et sine luctibus in Sion arce. . . .
Inde cremabitur, hinc solidabitur, ô Deus a te,
gens nova, grex novus, et numerus bonus ille bonorum,
Jerusalem petet, hic dat, ibi metet ordo piorum,
grex erit inclytus hoc patre praeditus, hoc duce nixus.
Qui tulit omnia sanguine noxia rex crucifixus.
Grex sacer ordine, splendidus agmine, lumine plenus,
vivet eo duce, qui tulit in cruce, rex Nasarenus.

[1] The Prologue shows that he has read the *Ars Poetica*, and he alludes to Virgil,
Cicero, Cato, Persius, Juvenal, and Lucilius. Mr. Raby (op. cit., p. 318) also attri-
butes to Bernard of Morlaas the well-known *Mariale* often attributed to Anselm or
Bernard of Clairvaux, beginning
ut jucundas cervus undas
aestuans desiderat
sic ad deum, fontem vivum
mens fidelis properat.

[2] In Neale's hymns 'Brief life is here our portion' (*Hymns Ancient and Modern*, 225),
'The world is very evil' (*A. & M.*, 226), 'For thee, O dear, dear country' (*A. & M.*,
227), and 'Jerusalem the golden' (*A. & M.*, 228). Neale himself said, 'I have no hesita-
tion in saying that I look on these verses of Bernard as the most lovely, in the same
way that the Dies Irae . . . is the most sublime, and the Stabat Mater . . . the most
pathetic of mediaeval poems' (quoted Hoskier, xiii). Neale's translation, however,
is less successful than a free version of part of the poem made by Swinburne in giving
an idea of the original (Mrs. Disney Leith, *Boyhood of Swinburne*, 1917, 33; quoted
Raby, 317).
O land without guilt, strong city safe built in a marvellous place
I cling to thee, ache for thee, sing to thee, wake for thee, watch for thy face:
Full of cursing and strife are the days of my life, with their sins they are fed,
Out of sin is the root, unto sin is the fruit, in their sins they are dead.
No deserving of mine can make answer to thine, neither I unto thee;
I a child of God's wrath, made subject to death, what good thing is in me?
Yet through faith I require thee, through hope I desire thee, in hope I hold fast,
Crying out, day and night, that my soul may have sight of thy joy at the last.

Pastus odoribus, interioribus, atque superno,
nectare dulcia protrahet ocia perpete verno,
per sacra lilia, perque virentia germina florum
exspaciabitur ac modulababitur ordo piorum,
pectora plausibus atque canoribus ora parabit,
dum sua crimina, lapsaque pristina stans memorabit . . .
O sine luxibus, ô sine luctibus, ô sine lite,
splendida curia, florida patria, patria vitae,
urbs Sion inclyta, patria condita littore tuto,
te peto, te colo, te flagro, te volo, canto, saluto.

The other arts that were practised at Cluny arose as
naturally out of the needs of the community as did its literature. The rule of St. Benedict decrees:[1]

'Artificers, if there be any in the monastery, shall practise their
special arts with all humility, if the abbot permit. But if any one of
them be exalted on account of his knowledge of his art, to the
extent that he seems to be conferring something on the monastery,
then such a one shall be deprived of his art, and shall not again
return to it, unless it hap that the abbot again order it, he being
humiliated.'

Peter the Venerable considered that the copying of books
was the pre-eminent monastic occupation:

'it is more noble', he wrote,[2] 'to set one's hand to the pen than
to the plough, to trace divine letters upon the page than furrows
upon the fields. Sow on the page the seed of the word of God,
and when the harvest is ripe, when your books are finished, the
hungry readers shall be satisfied by an abundant harvest.'

The copying of manuscripts had been practised at Cluny
long before his time. It was carried on in the lesser cloister,
which was reserved for meditation and quiet work.[3] The Precentor obtained the necessary parchment from the Chamberlain, and the Claustral Prior had it prepared for the use of
the scribes. They were allowed to go into the kitchen to
mix their ink at the fire and to dry their writings. The
uniformity of style that characterizes the extant manuscripts

[1] Cap. lvii; ed. Woelfflin, 55. The possibility of such products being sold is
envisaged, and the brethren are bidden to see that they are perfect, and that they are
sold at a reasonable price.
[2] *Epist.*, i. 20.
[3] At the Cluniac Priory of Wenlock there is a large room over the south aisle that
may have been used as a scriptorium (Cranage, 4).

Fig. XX. A CLUNIAC MINIATURE: THE ANNUNCIATION

Lectionary of Cluny, c. 1100

of the tenth, eleventh, and twelfth centuries that are known to come from Cluny, some of which are recorded to have been written there,[1] suggests that all those needed for the services and public reading of the abbey were produced in its own scriptorium; and the beauty of the writing and of the elaborately decorated initials shows that a high tradition of technical excellence was there maintained. In the time of Hugh, one brother, Durannus, devoted himself with such zeal to the copying of service books that when he died the Abbot, recognizing how well he had deserved of Cluny, had his anniversary instituted with double rites.[2] Under Pons de Melgueil the monk Peter, the precentor and head of the scriptorium, the Italian Opizon, and the German Albert of Treves collaborated to collate and copy a Bible that was considered unique in its beauty and accuracy.[3] Under Peter the works of Augustine, the poems of Prudentius, and the letters and treatise on miracles of Peter the Venerable are recorded to have been copied; and the work was considered to be so important that the copyists were even exempted from some of the regular Hours.

The manuscripts of Cluny were not only beautifully written, but were early enriched with decoration. A tenth-century manuscript[4] has pen-and-ink initials markedly Celtic alike in their form and in their interlaced ornament. Other manuscripts of the end of the same century[5] show initials formed of beasts and birds twisted into the shape of letters, for instance a peacock bent to form a C; and similar initials, this time coloured, adorn an antiphonal of about 1000[6]— a man holding two peacocks to form a letter M, a lion standing on its hind legs with paws outstretched to form a F (Fig. XVIII). Others in the same antiphonal are formed of elaborate interlacings, and the same style is further developed in a manuscript of the lives of saints written later in the century[7] (Fig. XIX), with plaited work, elaborate floriated

---

[1] e.g. B. M. Add. MS. 22820, Hrabanus Maurus, ordered by Maiol. For those in the Bibliothèque Nationale see Delisle, *Inventaire des Manuscrits de la Bibliothèque Nationale: fonds de Cluni*. For other works copied at Cluny see Sackur, ii. 328.
[2] Pignot, ii. 418.   [3] loc. cit.   [4] Bib. Nat. MS. nouv. acq. lat. 1460.
[5] Nouv. acq. lat. 1438 (Ambrose on Gospel of St. Luke) and nouv. acq. lat. 1461 (Hrabanus Maurus on Ecclesiasticus).   [6] Bib. Nat. lat. 1121.
[7] Bib. Nat. latin 3779. Cf. also Bib. Nat. nouv. acq. lat. 2247 (Sermons of Augustine).

scrolls, and strange contorted lions. The great lectionary of Cluny,[1] written about 1100, shows a further development: its noble pages are adorned with large miniatures to illustrate the lessons for the great Feasts—the Annunciation, the Crucifixion, and the Commission of the Apostles (Fig. XXI). The Annunciation (Fig. XX) is remarkable alike for its noble simplicity and for its almost mannered delicacy and grace.

Another art which grew as naturally out of the needs of the monastery as did the copying of manuscripts was that of music. At Cluny the art of chanting Gregorian music was brought to a high pitch of accomplishment, and there the musical traditions of Italy and France were fused to create the 'Roman-French' cycle which became the common heritage of Europe.[2] The musical treatises ascribed to Odo of Cluny are not by the great Abbot[3]; but the Cluniac Order produced a great musician in Remi of Auxerre, a monk of Saint-Germain, who inherited the tradition of Hrabanus Maurus from Heric of Auxerre. He wrote on musical rhythm, and is said to have given the sounds their names—buc, re, scembs, caemar, heth, uiche, asel.[4] While Abelard was living in retirement at Saint-Marcel, he wrote hymns and music both for that monastery and for the nunnery of which Heloïse was Abbess. One of these sequences begins:[5]

Mit-tit ad Vir-gi-nem Nonquem-vis An-ge-lum Sed for-ti -
- tu-di-nem Su-um Arch-ange-lum Am-a-tor ho - mi-nis.

The monastery libraries both of Cluny[6] and its dependent house of Saint-Martial-de-Limoges[7] included the treatise on

[1] Nouv. acq. lat. 2246.   [2] See Gastoué, 56.
[3] For them see Gerbert, *Scriptores*, i. 248 et seqq. They speak in laudatory terms of Abbot Odo's hymn to St. Martin: a self-praise of which he would never have been guilty. The treatises may perhaps be by another Odo of Cluny, who was Abbot of Saint-Maur-des-Fossés and died about 1030. See Gastoué, 81.
[4] Ibid.   [5] Gastoué, 94.   [6] See p. 99.
[7] Duplès-Agier, 351. Saint-Martial-de-Limoges played a part in the development of counterpoint. See Nef, 58.

FIG. XXI. A CLUNIAC MINIATURE: THE COMMISSION OF THE
APOSTLES
Lectionary of Cluny, c. 1100

music of Guy of Arezzo; and this, and the Gregorian tradition, seems to have governed its musical development, which was remarkable rather for accomplishment in execution than for creative originality. A typical Cluniac chant, used for the sequence in honour of St. Hugh, has been thus transcribed into modern notation: [1]

EGIS ae-terni re-gi-a sanc-tum hu-go-nem ho-di-

- e Re-ce-pit cum le-ti-ci-a in lar-go si-nu glo-ri-e. No-

- bi-lis ge-ne-re, sed mo-ri-bus no-bi-li-or, nichil de-ge-

- ne-rat. Cum Christo vi-ve-re vult, ut sit ge-ne-ro-si-or,

Chris-tum de-si-de-rat. Mundum habens in o-di-um, pu-rus

a pu-e-ri-ci-a. Clu-ni-a-ci ce-no-bi-um in-trat cum

de-i gra-ti-a. Le-ve de-i honus li-bens susti-nu-

[1] L'Huillier, *Vie de Saint Hugues*, p. 621. It is preserved in Bib. Nat. MS. fonds latin 17716, fol. 4, early thirteenth century. The chant is of the twelfth century.

- it & re - gu - la - ri - ter. Cunctis e - que bonus cunctis

com - pla - cu - it u - ni - versa - li - ter. Rector factus de -

-mum di - cti ce-no - bi - i, Cum Bar - iona re-mum sumpsit

re - mi - gi - i. Dum est ab-bas fa - ctus ce-pit os-ten- de -

- re Spi - ri - ta - les a - ctus ver-bo & o - pe-re. Ful-gens mi -

- ra - cu - lis re - no - vat om - ni - a. Pa-tet pre o - cu-lis

pre - sens ec - cle - si - a. Er- go pre-ce qua pos - su - mus,

san-cte Hu-go pa - ter e-gre - gi-e: Nos tu - i ser - vi, quae-

- su - mus, es - to tu-e me-mor ec-cle - si - e. Et qui-a me-tum

Fig. XXII. CLUNY: THE CAPITALS OF THE CHOIR: VIRTUES
AND SEASONS: PRUDENCE

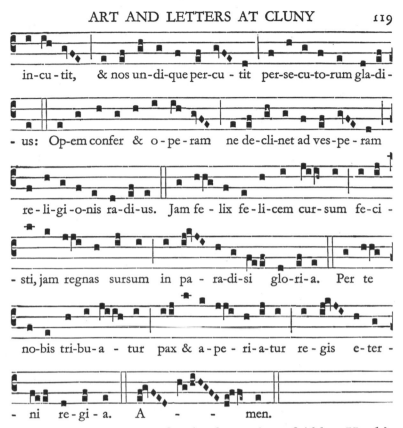

in-cu-tit, & nos un-di-que per-cu - tit per-se-cu-to-rum gla-di -

- us: Op-em confer & o-pe-ram ne de-cli-net ad ves-pe - ram

re-li-gi-o-nis ra-di-us. Jam fe - lix fe-li-cem cur-sum fe-ci -

- sti, jam regnas sursum in pa - ra-di-si glo-ri-a. Per te

no-bis tri-bu-a - tur pax & a-pe - ri-a-tur re - gis e-ter -

- ni re-gi - a. A - - men.

When the time came for the decoration of Abbot Hugh's great basilica, the Cluniac arts of literature, illumination, and music all played their part in its adornment. Radulphus Glaber, one of the most notable of the Cluniac writers, provided the literary source for the iconography of a series of its sculptured capitals. His *Historiarum libri V*, written about 1047, begin with a treatise on the quaternities of the world, of which the understanding will, he thinks, edify the mind and soul of those who meditate upon them.

'There are four gospels which build up in our minds the upper world; and the lower world is formed of the same number of elements. Similarly there are four virtues which rule all the rest and by their union form all others; and likewise we see our bodies provided with four senses, besides touch, which is less subtle than the rest and intended only to serve them. . . . We must also con-

sider with no less attention in accordance with the same system
the river which rises in the Eden of the East and divides into four
streams of renown. The first of them, the Phison, which is inter-
preted as the opening of the mouth, signifies Prudence that ever
pours out its salutary counsels in abundance. . . . The second, the
Gœon, or the chasm of earth, signifies Temperance, that virtue
which nourishes Chastity, and which prunes with a kindly hand
the evil growths of vice. The third is the Tigris, which flows
through the country of the Assyrians, a word which we translate
as "the Conduits"; it certainly signifies Fortitude, since it keeps off
all the vices of betrayal of trust to conduct man with God's help
to eternal bliss. The fourth, the Euphrates, whose name implies
abundance, evidently signifies Justice, which nourishes and re-
creates every soul truly devoted to it. These rivers then depict in
their mystic sense the image of the four virtues of which we have
spoken, as well as the image of the four Gospels. These same
virtues are not less clearly figured in the division of the duration
of the world into four ages.'

From the Creation to the Flood was the age of Prudence;
the time of Abraham and the patriarchs was the age of
Temperance; the time of Moses and the prophets was the
age of Fortitude; and the Christian era is the age of Justice.

The eight sculptured capitals of the choir at Cluny survive,[1]
the choir that was so beautiful that it was called *deambula-
torium Angelorum*.[2] Some of these show a striking parallelism
with the quaternities of Radulphus Glaber. On two of them
the four virtues appear: Prudence in helm and coat of mail,
(Fig. XXII), Justice with the whip of punishment in her
hand and a child before her,[3] Temperance and Fortitude.
The identification is made certain by the inscription round
the aureole of Prudence:

Dat cognoscendum prudentia quid sit agendum.

The two other faces of the capitals bear four other female

---

[1] In the Musée Ochier at Cluny. Their date has been much discussed. Professors
Kingsley Porter and Conant regard them as being of between 1088 and 1095; M.
Oursel would extend this dating to 1113; M. Bréhier would put them 'un peu après
1095'; M. Aubert 'vers 1120'; M. Deschamps in the second quarter or middle of the
twelfth century. This is not the place in which to enter on the details of the contro-
versy; but there seems a strong *prima facie* case for dating them about the time of the
consecration of the choir in 1095. Their effect cannot be fully appreciated now
unless their impost and the gorges to their columns be mentally added.

[2] *Vita Hugonis* by the monk Hugh (Marrier, 458).

[3] Only the child's foot survives. Mâle (*Art religieux en France au XII⁰ siècle*, p. 320)
says the figure is not Justice but Grammar; but this seems improbable.

Fɪɢ. XXIII. CLUNY: THE CAPITALS OF THE CHOIR: THE FOUR
RIVERS AND THE FOUR TREES

figures. Next to Prudence is a veiled woman dressed in a long robe and a floating mantle, holding a casket. On her aureole is written:

Ver primos flores primos aducit odores.

She is Spring; and opposite to her is Summer, likewise veiled.[1] The beginning of her inscription has been partly destroyed; the end reads:

. . . vens quas decoquit aestas.[2]

On the second capital Autumn and Winter accompany Fortitude and Temperance; none are inscribed.[3]

The third capital shows the four rivers that Radulphus describes: figures that represent them stand at each corner, with the waters flowing at their feet (Fig. XXIII). Between the rivers grow the four symbolic trees: the Apple of Knowledge, the Vine of Life, the Fig of the Fall, and the Almond of Resurrection.[4]

Two other capitals are harder to interpret: there are no inscriptions; the figures, instead of being set clearly like those of the other capitals, are merged in the conventional leafage of a classical Corinthian capital; and they have been seriously damaged. It is tempting to suppose that they may represent the two remaining[5] of Radulphus Glaber's quaternities, the Elements and the Senses. Two engaged capitals, it may be, were devoted to Radulphus's Four Ages of

---

[1] The figure is seriously damaged.

[2] The Abbé Prougnet suggests (*Annales archéologiques*, xxxviii) '[Falx resecat spicas fer]vens quas decoquit aestas'.

[3] The inscriptions were probably painted and have disappeared. The Abbé Terret (*La sculpture bourguignonne: Cluny*, 152) interprets the figures as representations of the Mechanical Arts.

[4] Aaron's rod blossomed and bore almonds, Numbers xvii. 31. Cf. Adam of St. Victor's hymn (Migne, *Patr. Lat.*, clxxxxvi. 1433):

Contemplemur adhuc nucem . . .
Nux est Christus; cortex nucis
circa carnem poena crucis;
testa, corpus osseum,
carne tecta Deitas,
et Christi suavitas
signatur per nucleum.

The tree on the capital is commonly thought to be an olive. This seems less appropriate.

[5] The symbols of the four Evangelists were represented on the portal of the abbey church and on the frescoes of the apse immediately above the scupltured capitals. See Mâle, *Art religieux du XIIᵉ siècle en France*, 384 et seq. For these and other quaternities, see Mâle, op. cit., 319.

R

History: at all events one that survives shows the Fall of Man and the Sacrifice of Abraham, two of the great events that divide his epochs; and the other may have shown Moses and the Annunciation.

The remaining two capitals of the choir are inspired by the other great Cluniac art of music. They represent the eight chants or tones of the liturgical use [1] that in their turn formed part of the harmonies of the universe. The first tone is represented by a young man with a lute, with an inscription on the edge of the aureole-like panel in which it is set:

> Hic tonus orditur modulamina musica primus.

The second tone is figured as a woman dancing and holding a cymbal, with the inscription:

> Subsequitur ptongus numero vel lege secundus (Fig. XXIV).

The third tone is represented by a young man with a six-stringed zither. Its inscription compares its rising movement with the Resurrection on the third day:

> Tertius impingit Christumque resurgere fingit.

The fourth tone is symbolized by a young man with three bells, one hanging from a rod, another at his elbow, and a third on the end of a wand.[2] Such bells were used at funerals, and symbolize the melancholy cadence of the fourth tone:

> Succedit quartus simulans in carmine planctus.

On the four sides of the second capital the remaining tones are figured and described. They are not set in panels like the first four, but appear among the foliage of the capital; the inscriptions are carved on a wide plain band that runs round the capital midway. The figures are much damaged, but the inscriptions are perfectly legible. That for the fifth tone runs

> Ostendit quintus quam sit quisquis tumet imus

—how low is fallen he who would raise himself—in allusion to its cadence.

---

[1] For a detailed study of them see Pouzet, 'Notes sur les chapiteaux de l'Abbaye de Cluny', in *Revue de l'art chrétien*, lxii, 1912, pp. 1, 104.
[2] Variants of this figure are sculptured at Vézelay and Autun.

Fig. XXIV. CLUNY: THE CAPITALS OF THE CHOIR: THE
SECOND TONE

The figure for the sixth tone plays a one-stringed guitar, with the inscription:

Si cupis affectum pietatis respice sextum.[1]

The seventh was represented blowing a trumpet, with the legend:

Insinuat flatum cum donis septimus almum

in allusion to the seven gifts of the Spirit. The eighth, with its tone of final peace, has the inscription,

Octavus sanctos omnes docet esse beatos,

in allusion to the eight beatitudes.

Nor were these capitals the only works of Art in the abbey church in which literature was married to sculpture. Before the High Altar stood a great candlestick eighteen feet high, made of gilt copper, set with crystals and beryls, made on the pattern of that which burnt before the Tabernacle,[2] with six branches and a central stem adorned with knops and lilies. It was inscribed:

Ad fidei normam voluit Deus hanc dare formam,
quae quasi praescriptum doceat cognoscere Christum:
de quo septenae sacro spiramine plenae
virtutes manant, et in omnibus omnia sanant.[3]

The other monastic art of the illumination of manuscripts likewise influenced the decoration of the Basilica. Certain details of the sculpture were designed in accordance with manuscript schemes: for example a capital in the surviving transept is carved with two rampant lions who turn to bite a leaf, that resemble similar lions in the initial letters of

[1] The number six was considered a symbol of perfection in the active life. See R. de Gourmont, *Le Latin mystique*, 161.

[2] Exodus xxv. 31. *Chronicon Cluniacense*; Marrier, 1640. It was the gift of Matilda, wife of Henry I of England. Bernard of Clairvaux describes it in his indictment of Cluniac splendour: 'Moreover we see candelabra standing like trees of massive bronze, fashioned with marvellous subtlety of art, and glistening no less brightly with gems than with the lights they carry.' Migne, *Patr. Lat.*, lxxii. 915; trans. G. G. Coulton, *Mediaeval Garner*, London, 1910, 68. Some idea of its form may be obtained from almost contemporary candlesticks of the same type still preserved in the cathedral of Brunswick and the collegiate church of Essen. Such a candlestick is recorded to have adorned the church built by St. Benedict at Aniane in 782 (Migne, *Patr. Lat.*, ciii. 363, quoted R. Graham, *English Ecclesiastical Studies*, p. 11).

[3] For other verse inscriptions on chalices and altars, see Albers, *Cons. Farf.*, 183.

manuscripts illuminated at Cluny.[1] But apart from such details, manuscript illumination itself provided the scheme and the technique for the great fresco that adorned the half-dome of the chancel apse: a figure of Christ[2] surrounded by the symbols of the Four Evangelists, with the four-and-twenty elders seated on their thrones below, as St. John saw them in his Apocalyptic Vision.[3] Miniatures illustrating this theme form some of the most striking illustrations of the early illuminated manuscripts of Beatus's commentary on the Apocalypse,[4] and the Christ in Majesty with the four beasts is commonly found in Missals.[5] The fresco of the abbey of Cluny has perished, but it is still possible to gain some idea of its scheme and style. The same subject is represented on rather later frescoes of which fragments survive in the Cluniac abbey of Vézelay and priory of Charlieu[6]; and in the Cluniac grange of Berzé, the favourite retreat of St. Hugh's old age, frescoes almost contemporary with the lost frescoes of the abbey still exist, that in their central figure of the seated Christ appear to reproduce on a smaller scale the central figure of the larger work[7] (Fig. XXV). Their beautiful warm colouring, with reddish ochres and purplish blues predominating, shows how the frescoes must have warmed and glorified the apse of the abbey. Nor were these the only paintings in the church; Peter the Venerable cites the scenes of the miracles of Christ in the Chapel of the Virgin as the finest in Burgundy.[8] The same beauty of colour was added to the sculptured decoration in soft stone[9]; but finer sculp-

---

[1] e.g. the Cluny Antiphonal (Bib. Nat. MS. fonds latin 1121), c. 1000, initial A on fol. 90.

[2] Philippe Bouché wrongly identifies the figure as God the Father, and many later writers have followed him; but the symbols of the Evangelists sufficiently indicate the figure to be Christ.

[3] Revelation iv. 2–8. Christ in Majesty was represented in sculpture on the tympanum of the abbey door. The theme reappears with variations on the doors of the Cluniac monastery churches of Moissac, Charlieu, Carennac, Ganagobie, Saint-Gilles, Vizille, and Mars.

[4] e.g. the *Beatus* of Saint-Sever, Bib. Nat. fonds latin 8878, fol. 121 *v* and 122.

[5] e.g. Missal of *c.* 1100 from Limoges: Bib. Nat. lat. 9483, fol. 58.

[6] Paintings of both of these showing them more clearly than the originals now do, belong to the Commission des Monuments Historiques at Paris.

[7] On these see Léonce Lex, Peintures murales de la chapelle du château des moines de Cluny a Berzé-la-Ville, in *Millénaire de Cluny*, ii. 248; and J. Virey, Saint Hugues et la chapelle de Berzé, in *Annales de l'Académie de Mâcon*, 1927.

[8] It was pulled down and reconstructed at the Renaissance (Pignot, ii. 504).

[9] I owe this information to the kindness of Professor Conant.

FIG. XXV. A CLUNIAC WALL-PAINTING: CHRIST ENTHRONED
Chapel of Berzé-la-Ville. First Years of the twelfth century

ART AND LETTERS AT CLUNY

ture in hard stone, such as the capitals of the ambulatory, was not coloured.

It is uncertain how far the abbey church and its treasures were actually built and made by the monks of Cluny. Hetzelon, a monk, is said to have supervised its construction[1]; and monkish hands may have contributed to its adornment. The *Consuetudines*, written for Farfa, describe a room near the novices' quarters where goldsmiths, and those engaged on leading glass might work, but there is nothing to show that these were monks, any more than the tailors and shoemakers for whom similar rooms were provided. Yet, even if the work was carried out by laymen, the whole inspiration of the art was monastic and Cluniac.

Bernard's indictment of the meaningless extravagance of Cluniac art[2] is too well known to need quotation; the study of the surviving and recorded ornaments of the abbey buildings reveals how little it was justified. Beautiful and splendid they were, but with a beauty and splendour made spiritual by their intellectual significance. The peculiar culture and the profound religious experience of the Cluniac community can nowhere have been more perfectly mirrored than in the abbey church where its members performed their chief work of prayer and praise.

[1] The usage was not uncommon in the Cluniac Order at the end of the eleventh century; the monk Alquier thus directed the building of Saint-Bertin, the monk Ponce that of Monstierneuf at Poitiers, and the Prior Gerard the construction of the first church at La Charité.

[2] Migne, *Patr. Lat.*, clxxii. 915. Translation in G. G. Coulton, *A Mediaeval Garner*, London, 1910, p. 68.

VII

CONCLUSION

SUCH was life at Cluny: a moderate interpretation of the Benedictine rule, warmed by charity and illumined by beauty in buildings, services, and music; setting psalmody in place of manual labour, cultivating the arts as well as theology; governed by tradition and custom in every detail of the day, yet saved from deadness alike by religious fervour and charitable deeds. To some minds the discipline at first appeared too light. Peter Damian stayed at the abbey as the guest of Abbot Hugh, and was struck by the contrast between the riches of the abbey and the monastic idea of poverty. 'How can they be holy and have holy men to lead them, they who live amid such abundance?' He asked Hugh to make the diet more austere: 'If for two more days in the week you could abstain from fat in your food, you who are so perfect in most other matters, would equal the anchorites in the mortification of the flesh.' But Hugh answered: 'Beloved father, before we try to increase our merits by increasing our abstinence, try yourself to endure our labours for a week, and then you will judge whether it is possible to add anything to our austerites. Until you have tasted such fare, you cannot know how much salt is needed to season it; until you have set your little finger to our task, you cannot truly know its extent and its burden.' So for a week Peter Damian followed the Cluniac Rule, and finding himself worn out at the end of it, admitted that the discipline was hard enough for a community to bear.[1] As late as the beginning of the thirteenth century Guiot de Provins declares:[2]

> Trop sont a Clini voir diant
> de ceu qu'il ont a covenant:
> toutes lor ententes i mettent;
> trop bien tiennent ce qu'il prometent—
> lor covinne äusse plus chier
> s'il fussent un po mensongier.
> Trop me tienent lor covenans
> qu'il me promettent la dedans:

[1] Marrier, 460.   [2] *Bible Guiot* (written between 1204 and 1209), line 1657.

il me promirent, sens mentir,
que quant je vodroie dormir
que il me covendroit vellier,
et quant je vodrie maingier
qu'il me feroient jeuner.
Plus me grieve trop de parler
qu'il me tollent que d'autre chose.
Il n'ont prou sens; nulz n'i repose;
toute nuit bruent a mostier—
mais ce m'i ai molt grant mestier
que je sai dormir en estant.
Per foi, travail i ai molt grant;
et quels repoz ont il lou jor
fors solement ou refroitor?
La nos aporte om oez pugnaiz
et feves a tout lou jambais.
Certes, sovent i sui iriez
por ceu que li vins est melleiz:
mal cuer me fait apres les oez
quar trop i ait dou boivre es buez.
Iqui rait villain convenant;
se j'en bovoie maintenant
un mois ne me feroit il ivre.
Millor morir i fait que vivre!

But as early as the time of Hugh, Adalberon of Laon was directing his satire against the customs of Cluny [1]; and the weary bickering between Cluniacs and Cistercians shows that the glory of Cluny was beginning to wane. After the death of Peter the Venerable, Cluny entered upon a period of decline that lasted for more than six hundred years, but of which the history is of little more than local interest. After his death there was a disputed election, and dissension and relaxation were rife within the Order; the Cistercian hostility continued active; the Papal Schism made the papal support of the Order a thing of little value; it happened that for some

[1] *Carmen ad Rotbertum Regem.* He declares that if a quiet monk were sent to Cluny he would come back in a few days wearing a great cap of bear's fur, a long robe drawn up to his knees and split in front, an embroidered baldric with a bow and arrows, a hammer and tongs, a sword, flint, steel, and tinder, with spurred shoes with curled-up toes, and would ask for his wife and children, declaring:

Miles nunc; monachus diverso more manebo;
Non ego sum monachus, iussu sed milito regis;
Nam dominus meus est rex Oydelo Cluniacensis.

time no Abbot held his office for long; and everything conspired to bring the glory of the Order to an end.[1] Hugh V,
who became Abbot in 1199, in 1200 issued new statutes for
the whole order, in which many of its characteristics were
renounced.[2] The ancient autocracy of the Abbot of Cluny
was surrendered; and constitutional government on Cistercian lines took its place. An annual General Chapter was
instituted,[3] to be attended by all the priors of the Order; and
two Abbots and two Priors were to be chosen to make
annually an inquisition into the conduct of the Abbot of
Cluny and the state of the abbey. In 1233 similar visitations
of the other houses of the Order were instituted.[4] Even so,
discipline was unsatisfactory; in 1231 Gregory IX had to
reform the Order and impose new regulations,[5] and a fresh
reformation had to be made by Nicholas IV in 1289. In the
next year the Visitors reported to the Chapter-General that
the abbey lacked wine, that the monks' food was ill-cooked,
and that the abbey owed more than fifty thousand *livres
tournois*.[6] The visitations of the fourteenth century show a sad
picture of decadence in morals and in customs.[7] The Spanish
dependencies one by one deserted Cluny for the Congregation of St. Benedict of Valladolid.[8] The Hundred Years' War
added to the difficulties of the abbey; the English manors
were lost, and many French priories were ruined. The
number of the monks at Cluny had been reduced to 120, and
was further reduced to 80; the usual pittances had to be
dropped.[9]

In 1457 a fresh stage of decline began with the appointment of Jean de Bourbon as Abbot. He was not even a
member of the Order, and was Abbot only in name. He

[1] In 1162 Pope Alexander III freed Vézelay from Cluniac jurisdiction, saying that
Cluny had fallen away from its earlier holiness and saintliness of life.
[2] Migne, *Patr. Lat.*, ccix. 882–96.
[3] The usage was confirmed by the Bull of Gregory IX in 1231.
[4] Bruel, in *Bibliothèque de l'École des Chartes*, 1873, xxxiv. 542.
[5] *Bull. Clun.*, 110; L. Auvray, *Régistre de Grégoire IX*, n. 745, p. 469. The last
moment of real splendour in medieval Cluny was the visit of Innocent IV accompanied by Saint Louis and Blanche of Castille in 1245. See Matthew Paris, ed.
Luard, iv. 484.   [6] Bruel, op. cit., 566.
[7] See Bruel, 'Visites des Monastères de l'Ordre de Cluny de la province d'Auvergne
aux XIIIᵉ et XIVᵉ siecle' in *Bibliothèque de l'École des Chartes*, 1891, lii. 64.
[8] Pignot, ii. 145.
[9] See A. Vaquier, 'Une réforme de Cluny en 1428', *Revue Bénédictine*, xxxv. 159;
R. Graham, *English Ecclesiastical Studies*, p. 73.

continued to be Bishop of Le Puy, but drew a fixed income from the abbey revenues. When he came to Cluny, he lived not in the abbey but in a fine house he built just outside its walls. At Paris he lived not in one of the Cluniac monasteries but in a splendid town-house, the Hôtel de Cluny.[1] In 1518 the monks of Cluny finally lost the right of electing their abbot. They elected one Jean de la Magdelaine, Bishop of Besançon, who had been Secretary to Margaret, Governess of the Netherlands, and was a known adherent of the Austrian House. Francis I was naturally offended. He cancelled the election, nominated Armand de Boissy, and declared that for the future the King should nominate the Abbot. Henceforward[2] the abbey was ruled by commendatory Abbots who took no real part in the life of the Order. In 1623 dissension once more crept within the Order, and split it into two congregations, 'de l'étroite observance' and 'de l'ancienne observance'.[3] Early in the seventeenth century a reforming movement gave fresh life to the Benedictine abbeys of France. They formed themselves into three great congregations of Cluny, Saint-Vanne, and Saint-Maur; and for a short time all these were united. Disunion, however, soon crept in, though the Congregation of Cluny still continued to exist.[4] In the middle of the eighteenth century it was felt that the medieval buildings of Cluny no longer answered the needs of the time, and all the monks' lodgings were rebuilt by the Claustral Prior Dom Dathoze.[5] Still the abbey declined; at the Revolution only forty-one monks remained.[6] The last High Mass was celebrated at Cluny on 25 October 1791, the anniversary of the consecration of the Basilica; and with the dispersion of the monks[7] the Order of Cluny came to an end. Even the great basilica did not long survive. In the summer of 1791 its bells were

[1] Now the Musée de Cluny. He was so complete a Humanist that he inscribed a verse of Virgil on an altar of Saint Eutrope (Champly, p. 222).
[2] On the later history of the abbey see Lorain, cap. xv et seqq.; Champly, chap. vii et seqq.; and Besse in *Revue Mabillon*, i. 5 èt seqq.
[3] The distinction lasted until the Revolution.
[4] See Lecestre, *Abbayes Prieurés et Couvents d'hommes en France . . . d'après les papiers de la Commission des Réguliers en 1768*. Paris, 1902.
[5] His buildings survive, and house the modern École des Arts et Métiers.
[6] Dom P. Denis. 'Quelques notes sur les derniers moines de l'abbaye de Cluny', in *Millénaire de Cluny*, ii. 116.
[7] One was living as late as 1837 (Ibid., 142).

melted for cannon, and on 29 November it was sacked by a revolutionary mob: the tomb of St. Hugh was profaned and defaced, the windows were broken, and the next day a great bonfire of wooden statues, books, manuscripts, and vestments was lit in the market-place. The abbey was left exposed to wind and weather, and on 21 April 1798, was sold by auction to three citizens of Mâcon for little more than two million francs. From sheer stupidity it was destroyed piecemeal: its deliberate destruction began on 16 July 1798, and did not end until 1811. The town, it is true, reacquired the eighteenth-century conventual buildings; but a road was made across the nave of the abbey church, the apse and the narthex were destroyed with gunpowder, and its glory was laid low.[1] Now a stable has been built within the sanctuary, an inn within the nave; only a single transept remains of the buildings begun by Hugh in 1088. Nowhere in Burgundy are images of the sainted abbots of Cluny still reverenced; but in that poor fragment of the basilica of their Order some breath of greatness, some echo of a devotion more magnificent than we know now, yet lingers; and there they will never be altogether forgotten.

[1] See E. Babelon in *Millénaire*, ii. 359; Conant, 'Five Old Prints of the Abbey Church of Cluny', in *Speculum*, iii, 1928, 402.

INDEX